FASHION AND APPAREL

From Artistic Expression to Sustainable Innovation

Eze celestine uwakwe

ISBN: 9798862012736

Cover design by: Art Painter
Library of Congress Control Number: 2018675309
Printed in the United States of America

*"Style is a way to say who you are without having to speak." -
Rachel Zoe*

CONTENTS

FOREWORD

In an age where trends come and go, and the fashion industry is constantly in flux, Eze Celestine Uwakwe has crafted a comprehensive and insightful exploration of this dynamic world. As the author of this book, I'm privileged to offer a foreword that sheds light on the importance of understanding the intricate tapestry of fashion and apparel.

Fashion is an ever-evolving art form, a cultural touchstone, and a powerful means of self-expression. It transcends the superficial and dives deep into the realms of identity, creativity, ethics, and sustainability. This book embarks on a journey through these dimensions, offering readers a chance to unravel the complexities and celebrate the beauty of fashion.

Eze Celestine Uwakwe's passion for fashion shines through every page, making this book not just a guide but a testament to the transformative power of style and innovation. As you immerse yourself in the following chapters, I encourage you to view fashion not merely as an industry but as a reflection of our times, a platform for self-discovery, and a canvas for positive change.

This comprehensive exploration is a testament to the author's dedication to shedding light on the multifaceted world of fashion. I invite you to embark on this journey with an open heart and a curious mind, ready to discover the magic that lies within the threads and fabrics that surround us every day.

Warm regards,

Eze celestine uwakwe

x

INTRODUCTION

Welcome to the captivating world of fashion and apparel, where artistry, culture, identity, ethics, sustainability, and technology intersect to create a vibrant tapestry of style and innovation. I'm Eze Celestine Uwakwe, and I'm honored to be your guide on this exploratory journey through the multifaceted realm of fashion.

Fashion is a language, a visual expression of who we are, what we believe in, and how we perceive the world. It transcends geographical borders, defies conventional norms, and invites us to celebrate diversity. In these pages, we will delve into the artistry of fashion as wearable art, explore its profound connection with culture and identity, and unravel the ethical and sustainable imperatives shaping its future.

The fashion and apparel industry is more than just clothing; it's a reflection of our times, a mirror to our values, and a catalyst for change. It embodies the fusion of creativity and commerce, tradition and innovation, history and future. Whether you are a seasoned fashion aficionado or someone taking their first steps into this world, I hope you find inspiration, knowledge, and a deeper appreciation for the art and industry of fashion within these chapters.

So, let us embark on this captivating journey together, as we navigate the intriguing landscape of fashion and apparel. The chapters that follow will offer insights, stories, and perspectives that illuminate the intricate web of threads that make up the world of fashion.

Welcome to "Fashion and Apparel: A Comprehensive Exploration."

PREFACE

In the ever-evolving world of fashion and apparel, where creativity knows no bounds and innovation is constant, this book serves as a comprehensive exploration of this dynamic and multifaceted industry. From the intersection of fashion with art, culture, and identity, to the pressing ethical and sustainability considerations, we embark on a journey through the vibrant and diverse landscape of fashion.

As someone deeply passionate about fashion and its influence on our lives, I am thrilled to share this exploration with you. Fashion is not merely about what we wear; it is a reflection of our values, a canvas for self-expression, and a powerful force that shapes our world. It has the ability to transcend cultural boundaries, challenge norms, and inspire change.

Through these pages, I aim to shed light on the beauty, artistry, and innovation that define the fashion and apparel industry. I also address the ethical and environmental challenges it faces and the promising solutions that lie ahead. Whether you are a fashion enthusiast, a budding designer, or simply curious about the world of fashion, I hope this book provides valuable insights and inspires you to view fashion as not just a commodity, but a form of art and a driver of positive change.

Thank you for embarking on this journey with me, and I invite you to immerse yourself in the captivating world of fashion and apparel.

Warm regards,

Eze Celestine Uwakwe

PROLOGUE

In the world of fashion and apparel, every garment tells a story. It whispers the secrets of its creation, reflects the culture from which it emerged, and hints at the aspirations of the wearer. This book is a collection of those stories—a journey through the artistry, culture, and innovation that define the ever-evolving realm of fashion.

As we dive into this exploration, I invite you to open your mind to the boundless creativity and diversity that fashion offers. From the runway to the streets, fashion is a mirror that reflects the complex interplay of individuality and society, tradition and progress, and aesthetics and ethics.

In the following chapters, we will traverse the landscapes of style and substance, delve into the nuances of identity and self-expression, and confront the ethical and environmental challenges that cast shadows over this glittering world. But amidst it all, we'll discover the resilience, ingenuity, and transformative potential that make fashion a force for good.

So, let these pages be your portal into a world where fabric becomes art, where clothing becomes a canvas for identity, and where fashion becomes a catalyst for change. As we journey through these chapters, remember that fashion is not just about what we wear—it's about who we are and who we aspire to be.

Eze Celestine Uwakwe

CHAPTER 1: THE EVOLUTION OF FASHION

Introduction

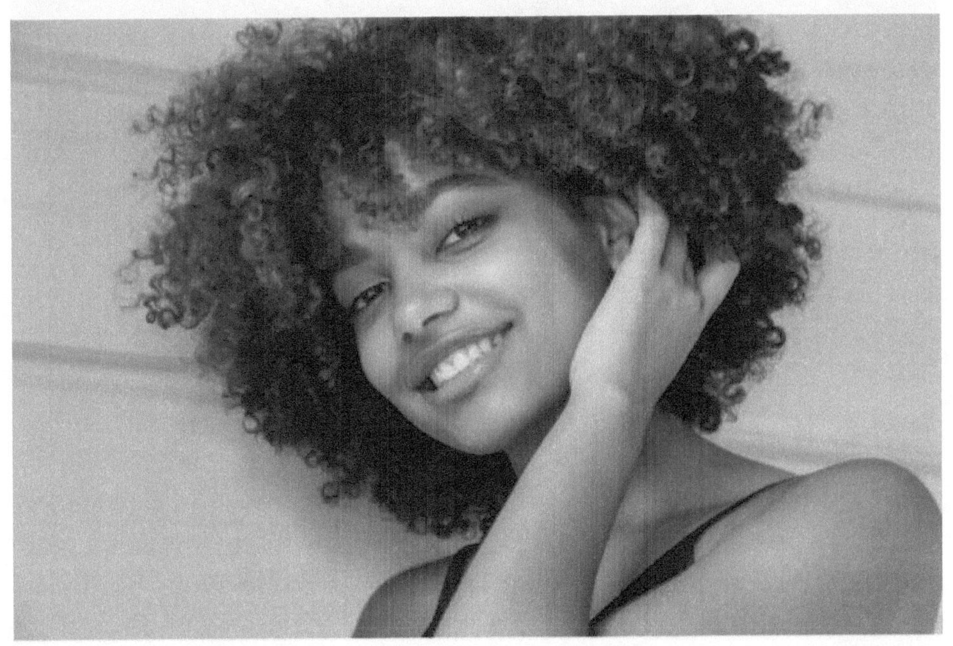

Fashion, the ever-changing tapestry of clothing and style, has captivated humanity for centuries. It's a form of self-expression, a reflection of culture, and a testament to the creativity of humanity. In this chapter, we will embark on a journey through time, exploring the fascinating evolution of fashion, from its humble origins to its current status as a global phenomenon.

Historical Overview

Ancient Civilizations and Early Clothing Styles

The story of fashion begins in the annals of ancient civilizations. In Egypt, clothing was not just a matter of utility; it held deep symbolic meaning. The flowing white robes of the Pharaohs symbolized purity and divinity, while intricate jewelry and headdresses were markers of status.

In ancient Greece and Rome, fashion was a blend of practicality and aesthetics. Togas and tunics were the norm, but the cut, color, and adornments of these garments signified social class and rank.

Medieval and Renaissance Fashion

The Middle Ages ushered in an era where religion and social status dictated clothing choices. In Europe, sumptuary laws were enacted to regulate what individuals could wear based on their class and occupation. The medieval period was marked by heavy, layered garments, with knights donning suits of armor for protection.

The Renaissance period witnessed a dramatic shift in fashion.

Tailoring became an art, with clothing designed to accentuate the human form. Intricate embroidery, luxurious fabrics, and the famous codpiece became symbols of wealth and refinement.

The Emergence of the Modern Fashion Industry

The Renaissance laid the foundation for the modern fashion industry. Tailors and dressmakers began to create clothing for a broader clientele. In the 17th century, France became a fashion hub, and the court of Louis XIV set trends for Europe.

The French Revolution, with its call for equality, disrupted the world of fashion. Extravagance gave way to simpler, more practical clothing. The birth of the "little black dress" during this era marked a turning point in fashion history.

Key Fashion Periods

The 19th Century: From Corsets to Crinolines

The 19th century brought with it new challenges and opportunities for fashion. The Victorian era was characterized by modesty, corsets, and hoop skirts. Women's fashion was defined by hourglass silhouettes, while men favored tailcoats and cravats.

The Industrial Revolution revolutionized clothing production. Ready-to-wear clothing became more accessible to the masses, paving the way for the mass-produced fashion we know today.

The Roaring Twenties: Flappers, Jazz, and the Rise of Ready-to-Wear

The 1920s marked a dramatic departure from the constraints of previous eras. The Roaring Twenties was a time of exuberance, characterized by flapper dresses, bobbed hair, and bold makeup. Jazz music and the rise of cinema played a significant role in shaping fashion and popular culture.

Fashion Icons and Innovators

Fashion history is replete with iconic figures who left an indelible mark on the industry.

Coco Chanel: The Woman Who Revolutionized Women's Fashion

Coco Chanel, a visionary designer, challenged the conventions of women's fashion in the early 20th century. Her revolutionary designs, including the "little black dress" and Chanel No. 5 perfume, epitomized simplicity and sophistication. Chanel's enduring legacy continues to influence modern fashion.

Yves Saint Laurent: Bringing High Fashion to the Streets

Yves Saint Laurent democratized fashion by bringing high-end design to the masses. He pioneered the tuxedo jacket for women, challenging traditional gender norms and empowering women to embrace menswear-inspired fashion.

Alexander McQueen: Pushing the Boundaries of Fashion and Art

Alexander McQueen was a maverick who blurred the lines between fashion and art. His provocative runway shows, like "Highland Rape" and "Plato's Atlantis," challenged societal norms and pushed the boundaries of what fashion could be. His avant-garde designs continue to inspire and shock the world.

Conclusion

In this chapter, we've explored the rich tapestry of fashion's evolution, from its origins in ancient civilizations to the revolutionary designs of modern fashion icons. Fashion is a dynamic, ever-evolving art form that reflects the spirit of its time.

It's a testament to our creativity, individuality, and our unceasing desire to express ourselves through clothing. As we delve deeper into the world of fashion in the following chapters, we'll discover how it continues to shape our lives and culture in profound ways.

CHAPTER 2: UNDERSTANDING STYLE

Introduction

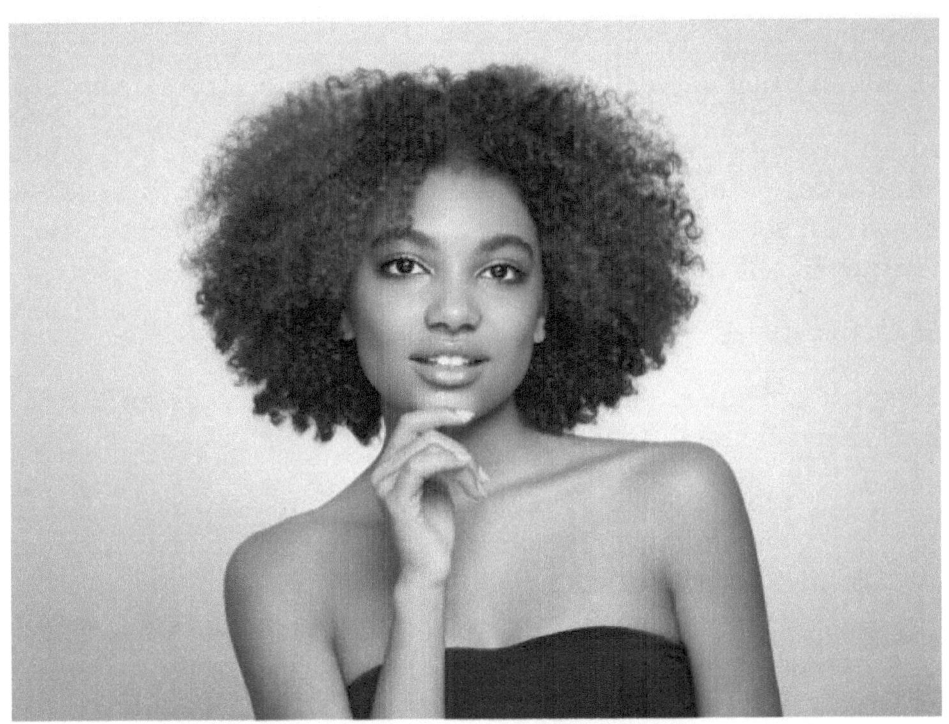

In the world of fashion, style is the unique language through which individuals express themselves. It's the distinct mark of personality that goes beyond fleeting trends and mass-produced clothing. In this chapter, we will explore the concept of style, its role in shaping identity, and how it intertwines with the ever-changing landscape of fashion.

Defining Personal Style

Exploring Personal Style

Style is more than just clothing; it's an extension of one's personality. It's the way we communicate who we are without uttering a word. When you look at someone, their style can tell you about their values, tastes, and even their mood on a given day.

At its core, personal style is about authenticity. It's about embracing what makes you unique and using clothing as a canvas for self-expression. Understanding your personal style is a journey of self-discovery and self-acceptance.

Style Archetypes

Personal style often falls into recognizable archetypes, each with its distinct characteristics:

> Classic: Timeless elegance and sophistication.
> Bohemian: Free-spirited and eclectic, often drawing from different cultures.
> Minimalist: Clean lines, simplicity, and a "less is more" philosophy.
> Eclectic: A mix of various styles, blending the unexpected.
> Vintage: Nostalgic and inspired by past eras.

Identifying your style archetype can help you refine your fashion choices and create a more cohesive wardrobe. However, it's important to note that most individuals exhibit a blend of these archetypes, and personal style is fluid.

Fashion vs. Style

Fashion vs. Style: A Nuanced Distinction

Fashion and style are often used interchangeably, but they represent distinct concepts. Fashion is the broader industry encompassing clothing, accessories, and trends, while style is the unique way individuals interpret and wear fashion.

The Relationship Between Fashion and Style

Fashion plays a significant role in influencing style choices. Runway shows, fashion magazines, and social media platforms showcase the latest trends and designs, inspiring individuals to incorporate these elements into their personal style.

Conversely, personal style can influence fashion trends. Style icons and fashion-forward individuals can popularize specific looks and aesthetics, causing them to become mainstream.

Building a Stylish Wardrobe

The Foundation of a Stylish Wardrobe

A stylish wardrobe begins with essential pieces that form the foundation of your style. These timeless items are versatile, enduring, and serve as the building blocks for various outfits. For women, this might include a little black dress and well-fitted jeans, while men might opt for a classic suit and quality white shirts.

Creating a Capsule Wardrobe

A capsule wardrobe is a curated collection of clothing items that mix and match seamlessly, allowing for a multitude of outfits with fewer pieces. The principles of a minimalist wardrobe involve decluttering your closet and investing in high-quality, versatile garments.

The Art of Mixing and Matching

One key to a stylish wardrobe is the ability to mix and match your clothing items to create diverse looks. Accessories, such as scarves, belts, and jewelry, can transform an outfit. Experimenting with layering, color combinations, and textures can also elevate your style.

Conclusion

Understanding style is a personal journey of self-expression and authenticity. Your style reflects your unique identity and is a powerful tool for communicating who you are to the world. As we delve deeper into the world of fashion and style in the following chapters, we'll explore how these concepts continue to evolve and influence our lives in profound ways.

CHAPTER 3: THE FASHION INDUSTRY TODAY

Introduction

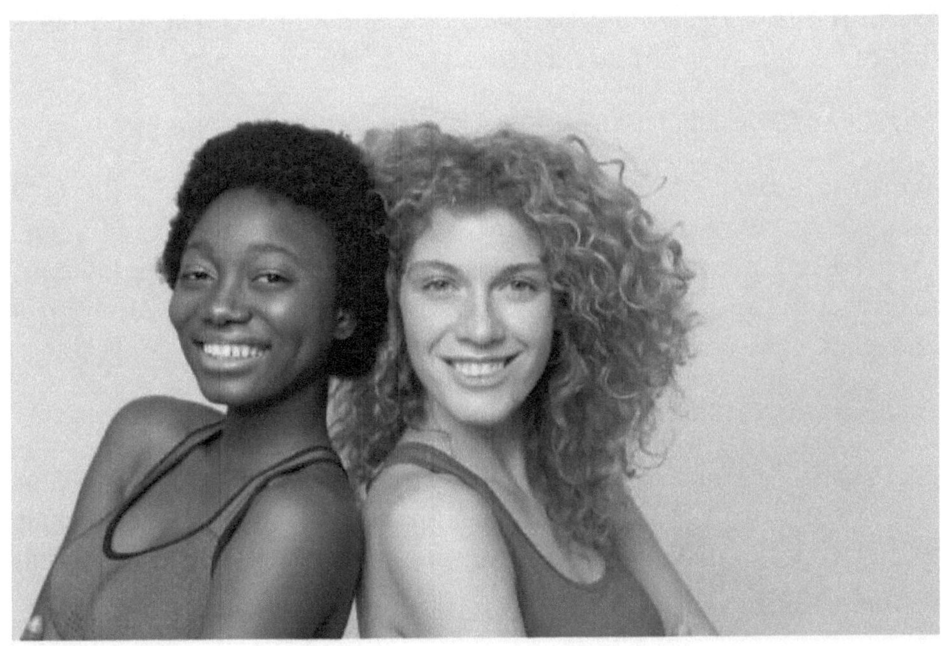

The fashion industry is a dynamic and ever-evolving landscape that reflects the tastes, values, and aspirations of society. In this chapter, we will explore the contemporary state of the fashion industry, examining the factors that shape it, the key players, and the trends that define the fashion landscape today.

Fashion Trends and Forecasting

The Rapid Pace of Change

Fashion is inherently ephemeral, with trends coming and going at a rapid pace. What's "in" one season may be "out" the next. The fashion industry's ability to anticipate and adapt to these shifts is one of its defining characteristics.

The Role of Trend Forecasting

Trend forecasting is a vital part of the fashion industry. Experts analyze various sources, from runway shows to street style, to predict upcoming trends. These forecasts influence design, production, and purchasing decisions across the fashion supply chain.

Fast Fashion vs. Sustainable Fashion

Fast fashion, characterized by its rapid production and low-cost items, has dominated the industry in recent decades. However, it has also come under scrutiny for its environmental and ethical implications.

Conversely, the sustainable fashion movement has gained momentum, with consumers and brands alike prioritizing eco-friendly and socially responsible practices. The shift toward sustainability is a defining trend of the contemporary fashion industry.

Fashion Weeks and Runway Shows

The Fashion Calendar

Fashion weeks, held in major fashion capitals like New York, Paris, Milan, and London, set the tone for the industry. These events occur twice a year, showcasing upcoming collections from renowned designers and emerging talents.

The Evolution of Runway Shows

Runway shows have transformed in the digital age. While they were once exclusive events for industry insiders, they are now often live-streamed to a global audience. The democratization of fashion weeks has expanded their reach and impact.

Fast Fashion vs. Sustainable Fashion

Fast Fashion: The Pros and Cons

Fast fashion brands like Zara, H&M, and Forever 21 have made trendy clothing affordable and accessible to the masses. However, their rapid production cycles contribute to issues like overconsumption, environmental pollution, and labor exploitation.

Sustainable Fashion: A Growing Movement

Sustainable fashion focuses on reducing the industry's ecological footprint and ensuring ethical labor practices. It encompasses eco-friendly materials, fair wages for workers, and transparency in the supply chain. Sustainable fashion brands aim to balance style and ethics.

Conclusion

The fashion industry today is a complex and multifaceted ecosystem, marked by rapid trends, dynamic fashion weeks, and a growing emphasis on sustainability. As we continue our exploration of fashion and style in the following chapters, we'll delve deeper into the impact of these trends and the diverse facets of the contemporary fashion world.

CHAPTER 4: WARDROBE ESSENTIALS

Introduction

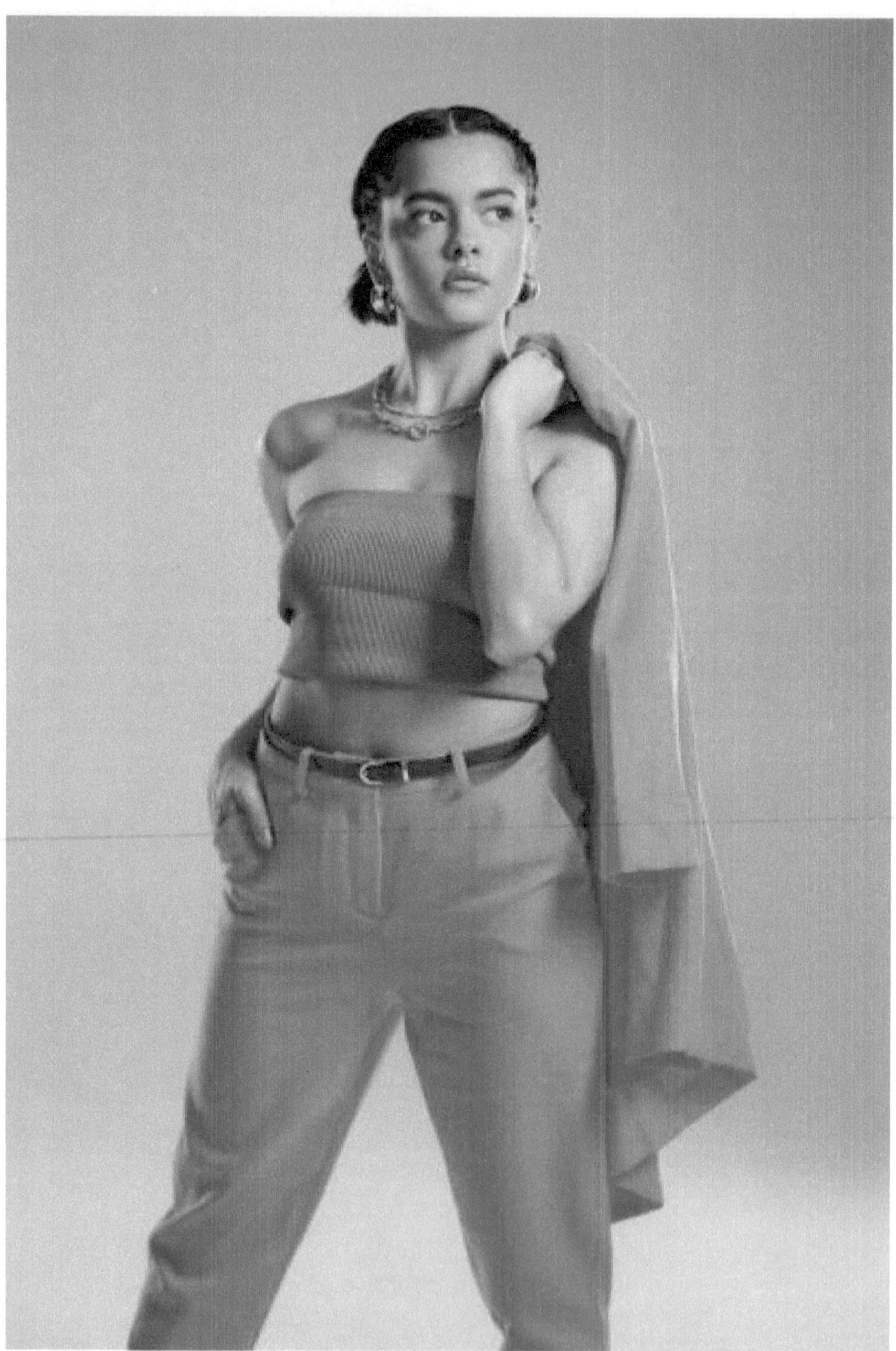

A stylish wardrobe begins with a solid foundation of essential pieces that are versatile, timeless, and adaptable to a variety of occasions. In this chapter, we will explore the core elements of a stylish wardrobe, offering guidance on selecting and maintaining these items.

Must-Have Clothing Items

For Women

The Little Black Dress: A classic LBD is a versatile staple that can transition from day to night with ease.

Well-Fitted Jeans: A great pair of jeans that fit perfectly is a wardrobe essential. Opt for a timeless style in a dark wash.

White Button-Down Shirt: A crisp white shirt is a versatile piece that can be dressed up or down for various occasions.

Tailored Blazer: A well-cut blazer instantly elevates any outfit, making it suitable for work, events, or casual outings.

Comfortable Flats and Heels: A pair of comfortable flats and classic heels are essential for both comfort and style.

For Men

White Dress Shirt: A white dress shirt is a versatile piece that can be worn with suits, blazers, or casually with jeans.

Navy Suit: A navy suit is a versatile choice suitable for business meetings, formal events, or a sharp everyday look.

Dark Jeans: Dark, well-fitted jeans can be dressed up with a blazer or dressed down with a t-shirt.

Leather Dress Shoes: Invest in quality leather dress shoes in black and brown that can be worn with various outfits.

T-Shirts and Polos: Basic t-shirts and polos in neutral colors are versatile and comfortable for everyday wear.

Accessorizing for Impact

For Women

- Statement Necklace: A bold statement necklace can transform a simple outfit into something eye-catching.
- Quality Handbag: Invest in a quality handbag that complements your style and is functional for your needs.
- Scarf: Scarves add texture and color to your outfits and can be worn in multiple ways.

For Men

- Wristwatch: A classic wristwatch is a timeless accessory that adds sophistication to any look.
- Leather Belt: A well-made leather belt in black and brown is essential for holding your outfit together.
- Pocket Square: For formal occasions, a pocket square adds a touch of elegance to a suit jacket.

Dressing for Different Occasions

For Women

- Work Attire: Tailored blouses, pencil skirts, and well-fitted trousers are staples for professional settings.
- Casual Wear: Jeans, t-shirts, and comfortable flats are perfect for everyday errands and outings.
- Evening Wear: A little black dress, statement heels, and elegant accessories are ideal for formal events.

For Men

- Business Attire: Crisp dress shirts, tailored suits, and polished dress shoes are suitable for the workplace.
- Casual Wear: Dark jeans, button-down shirts, and sneakers

or loafers are comfortable for everyday activities.

- Formal Wear: A well-fitted tuxedo or formal suit, along with a bow tie or necktie, is essential for black-tie events.

Conclusion

Wardrobe essentials are the building blocks of a stylish and versatile clothing collection. These timeless pieces provide the foundation for a wide range of outfits, allowing you to express your personal style with confidence. As we continue our exploration of fashion and style in the following chapters, we'll delve into more specific aspects of dressing and accessorizing.

CHAPTER 5: FASHION ON A BUDGET

Introduction

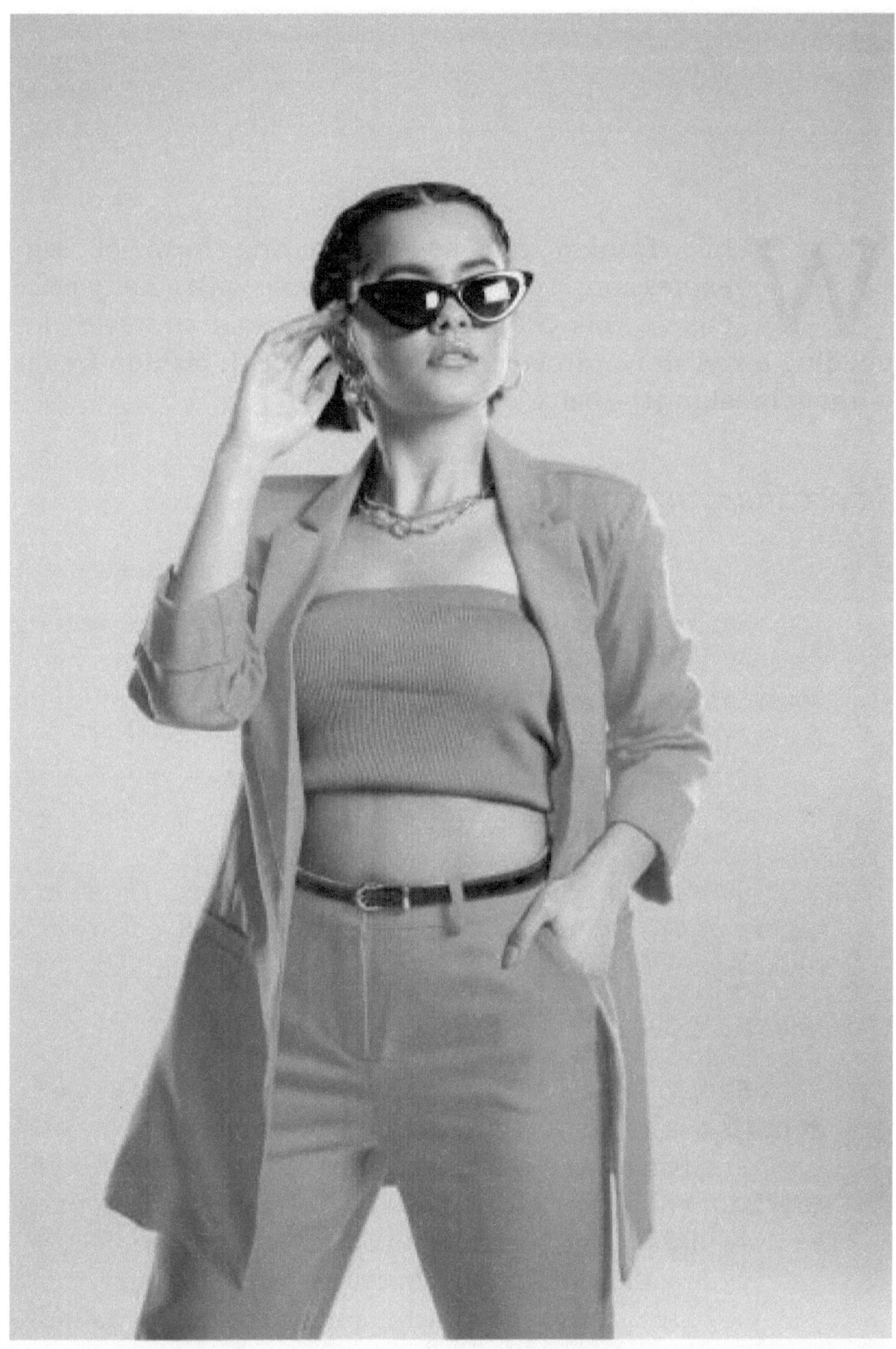

While fashion can be an exciting form of self-expression, it doesn't have to come with a hefty price tag. In this chapter, we will explore strategies for building a stylish wardrobe and keeping up with fashion trends without breaking the bank.

Smart Shopping Tips

Understanding Your Budget

Set a Budget: Determine how much you're willing to spend on fashion each month or season. This helps you manage your finances and make informed purchasing decisions.

Prioritize Essentials: Allocate a portion of your budget to wardrobe essentials and versatile pieces that will get frequent use.

Save for Special Purchases: If you have your eye on a higher-priced item, create a separate savings fund to work toward your fashion goals.

Shopping Strategies

Shop Off-Season: Buying clothing at the end of a season or during sales can save you a significant amount.

Thrifting and Consignment: Thrift stores and consignment shops offer affordable, unique fashion finds. Explore vintage and secondhand options.

Online Discounts: Look for online sales, discount codes, and cashback offers when shopping from your favorite brands.

Thrift Store Treasures

The Thrifting Experience

Exploring Thrift Stores: Thrift stores are treasure troves of unique and budget-friendly fashion items. Spend time browsing to discover hidden gems.

Try Before You Buy: Check the condition and fit of thrifted clothing. Many thrift stores have fitting rooms to ensure the items meet your needs.

Repurposing and DIY

Repurposing Clothing: Get creative by altering or repurposing thrifted pieces to fit your style. You can transform a dated garment into a trendy fashion statement.

DIY Projects: Explore DIY fashion projects, such as customizing jeans, creating tie-dye shirts, or embellishing accessories. These projects are both fun and cost-effective.

Fashion on a Shoestring: Budget-Friendly Brands

Affordable Brands: Many fashion brands offer budget-friendly lines without compromising style and quality.

Fast Fashion: While fast fashion comes with ethical and environmental concerns, it's an option for staying trendy on a budget. Be mindful of the impact and consider more sustainable choices when possible.

Conclusion

Fashion on a budget is entirely achievable with a bit of creativity, planning, and smart shopping. By setting a budget, exploring thrift stores, and being strategic about your purchases, you can build a stylish wardrobe without overspending. In the following chapters, we'll continue to explore ways to make fashion accessible and sustainable for everyone.

CHAPTER 6: FASHION AND CULTURE

Introduction

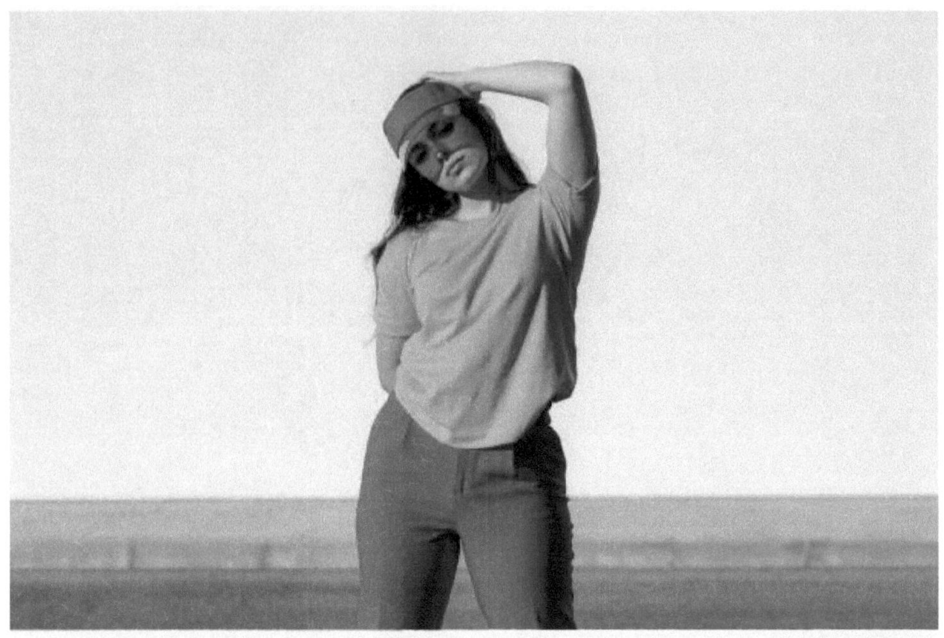

Fashion is not just about clothing; it's a mirror reflecting the cultural, societal, and historical context of the time. In this chapter, we will explore the profound impact of culture on fashion, examining how different cultures have influenced and continue to shape the world of style.

Cultural Influences on Fashion

Egyptian Influence

Ancient Egypt: The ancient Egyptians greatly valued clothing for its symbolism. Garments like the pharaoh's headdress and the pleated linen kilt conveyed status, religion, and mythology.

Egyptian Revival: Throughout history, periods of "Egyptian revival" have seen fashion incorporating Egyptian motifs, such as scarab beetles and hieroglyphics.

Indian and South Asian Influence

Bollywood Fashion: The vibrant and elaborate costumes in Bollywood films have inspired Indian and global fashion trends. Traditional Indian garments like sarees and kurta-pajamas have also made their mark.

Henna and Jewelry: Henna tattoos and intricate jewelry designs are part of South Asian culture and have become popular fashion accessories worldwide.

Japanese Influence

Kimono: The kimono is a symbol of Japanese culture, known for its elegance and intricate craftsmanship. It has influenced Western fashion, inspiring designers with its minimalism and clean lines.

Street Style: Japanese street style, characterized by bold and avant-garde fashion choices, has had a significant impact on global fashion trends.

Ethnic and Tribal Fashion

African Textiles: African textiles like Ankara and Kente have gained international recognition for their vibrant patterns and cultural significance.

Indigenous Fashion: Indigenous communities around the world contribute to fashion through traditional clothing, beadwork, and unique patterns that reflect their heritage.

Appropriation vs. Appreciation

Cultural Appropriation: The controversial issue of cultural appropriation arises when elements of one culture are borrowed or copied by individuals from a dominant culture, often without proper understanding or respect.

Cultural Appreciation: Cultural appreciation, on the other hand, involves acknowledging and respecting the cultural origins of fashion and celebrating diversity through style.

Conclusion

Fashion is a tapestry woven with threads of culture, history, and identity. As we've explored in this chapter, different cultures have played a significant role in shaping fashion trends and style. It's essential to recognize and appreciate these influences while being mindful of the impact of cultural appropriation. In the following chapters, we'll delve into how fashion continues to evolve and adapt in a globalized world.

CHAPTER 7: FASHION AND SELF-EXPRESSION

Introduction

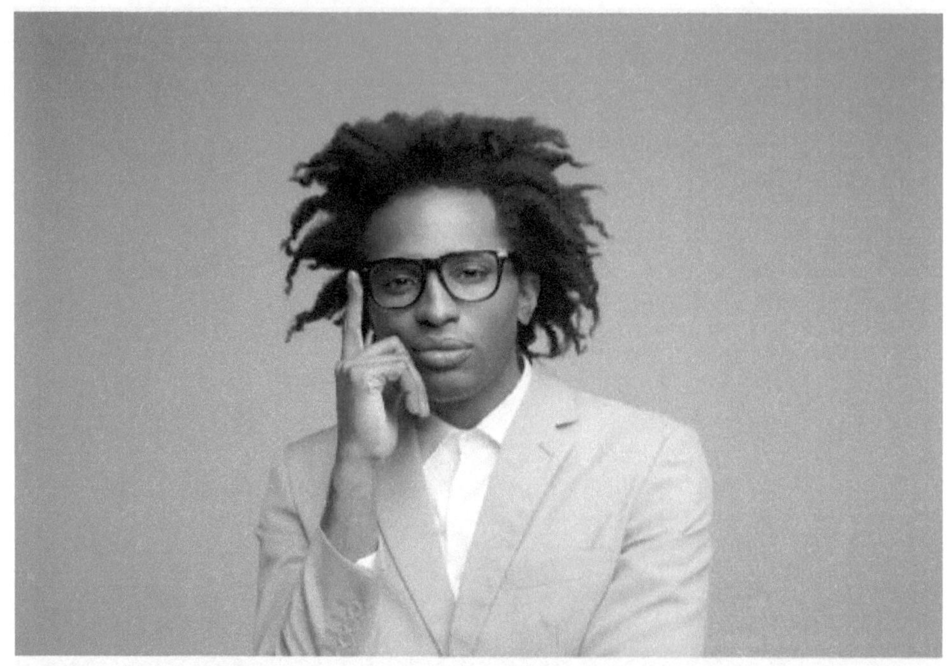

Fashion is not just about the clothes we wear; it's a form of self-expression that allows us to communicate our identity, values, and emotions to the world. In this chapter, we will explore how fashion serves as a powerful tool for self-expression and how it intersects with topics like gender, subcultures, and body image.

Gender and Fashion

Gender Norms and Fashion

Historical Gender Norms: Throughout history, clothing has been used to reinforce and sometimes challenge traditional gender norms. From corsets to suits, fashion has often been gendered.

Gender-Neutral Fashion: In recent years, there has been a movement towards gender-neutral or gender-inclusive fashion, with designers creating clothing that transcends traditional gender boundaries.

Subcultures and Identity

Subcultural Fashion Movements

Punk Fashion: The punk subculture embraced DIY aesthetics, with ripped clothing, leather jackets, and iconic punk accessories like studded belts and band patches.

Goth Fashion: Goth fashion is known for its dark and dramatic style, characterized by black clothing, heavy makeup, and a fascination with the macabre.

Street Style and Urban Fashion

Hip-Hop Fashion: Hip-hop culture has had a profound impact on fashion, with baggy jeans, oversized shirts, and sneakers becoming iconic elements of urban fashion.

Skater Culture: Skateboarding culture has influenced streetwear fashion, emphasizing comfort, loose-fitting clothing, and graphic tees.

The Role of Tattoos and Piercings

Body Modification: Tattoos and piercings are forms of body modification that have become mainstream fashion expressions. They can convey personal stories, beliefs, or simply aesthetics.

Tattoo Artistry: Tattoo artists have gained recognition as both artists and fashion influencers, with their work often featured in fashion and lifestyle magazines.

Conclusion

Fashion is a canvas through which we paint our identities, values, and emotions. It allows us to challenge and transcend societal norms, express our individuality, and find belonging in various subcultures. In this chapter, we've explored how fashion intersects with gender, subcultures, and body modification as powerful forms of self-expression. In the following chapters, we'll continue to unravel the multifaceted world of fashion and style.

Chapter 8: The Business of Fashion

Introduction

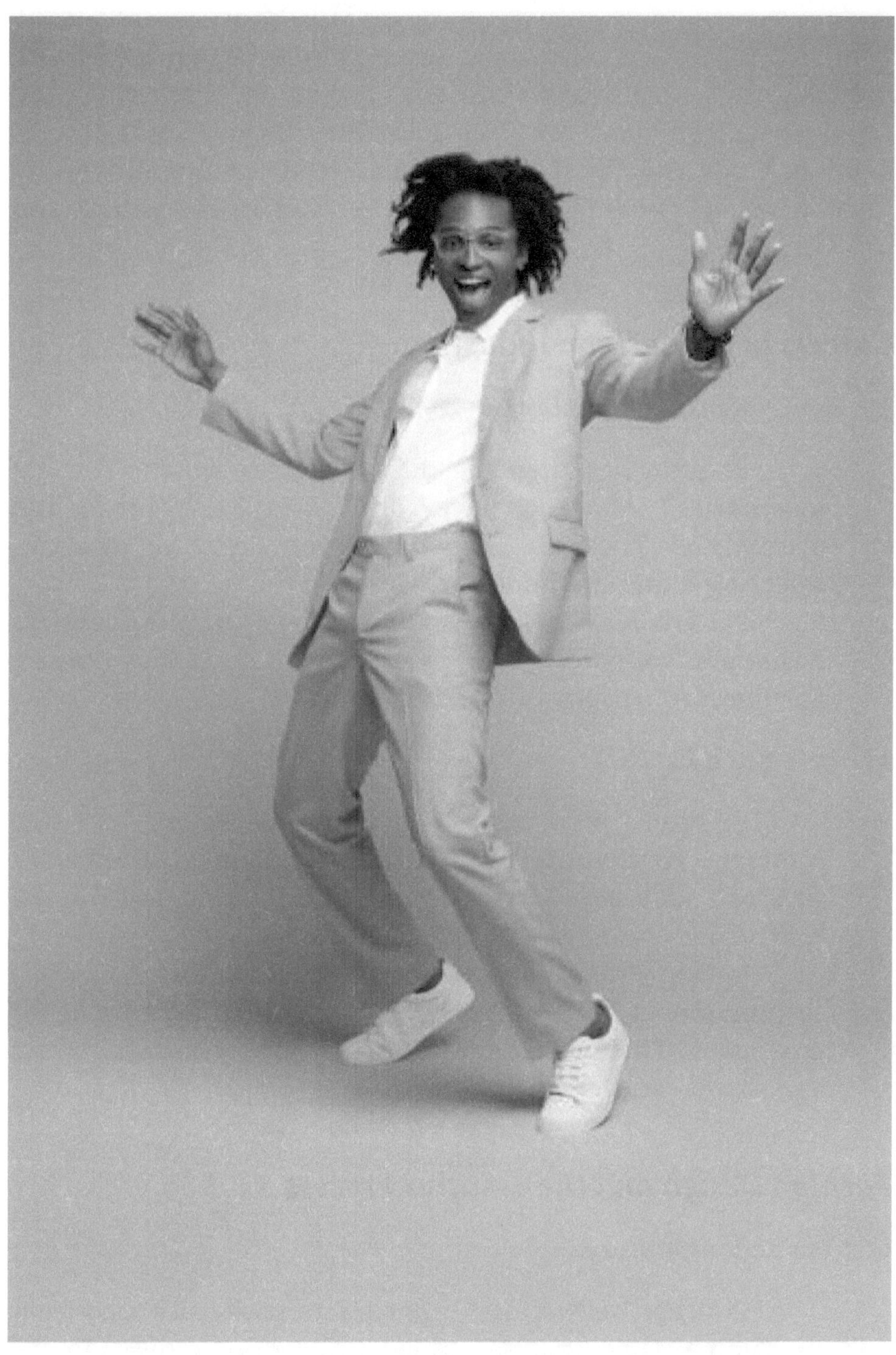

Behind the glamour of fashion lies a complex and multifaceted industry that encompasses design, production, marketing, and retail. In this chapter, we will delve into the business side of fashion, exploring the careers it offers, the creative process of fashion design, and the strategies involved in marketing and branding.

Careers in the Fashion Industry

Fashion Design and Production

Fashion Designers: Fashion designers are the creative visionaries who conceive and create clothing and accessories. They are responsible for sketching designs, selecting materials, and overseeing the production process.

Pattern Makers and Tailors: Pattern makers translate designers' sketches into patterns, while tailors ensure garments fit perfectly through alterations.

Marketing and Retail

Fashion Marketers: Fashion marketers develop strategies to promote and sell fashion products. They work in areas such as advertising, public relations, and digital marketing.

Retail Professionals: Retail professionals manage fashion stores, ensuring a seamless shopping experience for customers. This includes roles such as visual merchandisers and store managers.

Fashion Design and the Creative Process

Concept and Inspiration

Concept Development: Designers start with a concept or theme that inspires their collection. This can be influenced by art, culture, history, or personal experiences.

Sketching and Prototyping: Designers sketch their ideas and create prototypes to bring their vision to life.

Materials and Production

Material Selection: Choosing the right fabrics and materials is crucial to achieving the desired look and feel of a collection.

Production and Manufacturing: Garments are produced, often in collaboration with manufacturers, factories, or artisans who specialize in specific techniques.

Marketing and Branding

Building a Brand Identity

Branding: Developing a brand identity involves creating a unique and recognizable image, logo, and messaging that resonate with the target audience.

Storytelling: Effective storytelling through advertising and marketing campaigns helps consumers connect with a brand on a personal level.

Marketing Strategies

Digital Marketing: In the age of the internet, digital marketing plays a vital role in reaching a global audience through social media, e-commerce, and influencer collaborations.

Sustainability in Branding: Brands that prioritize sustainability and ethical practices are gaining prominence, reflecting a growing consumer awareness of environmental and social issues.

Conclusion

The fashion industry is not just about aesthetics; it's a vast and intricate world that offers a multitude of career paths, from design and production to marketing and retail. Understanding the creative process of fashion design and the strategies involved in marketing and branding is essential for anyone interested in this dynamic field. In the following chapters, we'll continue our exploration of the multifaceted world of fashion and style.

CHAPTER 9: FASHION AND TECHNOLOGY

Introduction

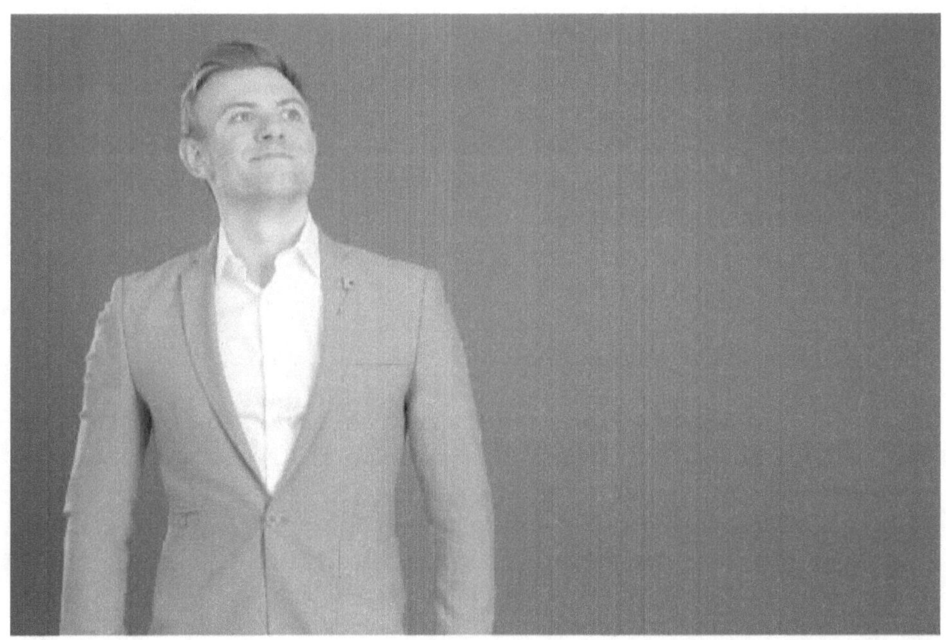

Fashion and technology are two seemingly disparate fields that have increasingly intertwined in the modern era. In this chapter, we will explore the fascinating intersection of fashion and technology, from wearable tech to sustainable innovations.

Wearable Technology

The Rise of Wearables

Smartwatches: Smartwatches like the Apple Watch have seamlessly integrated technology into everyday fashion, offering functionalities like fitness tracking and notifications.

Wearable Fitness Tech: Wearable fitness trackers monitor health metrics and activity levels while blending seamlessly with athletic wear.

Fashion and Tech Collaboration

Designer Tech Collaborations: High-end fashion designers have partnered with tech companies to create wearable tech that combines style and functionality.

Fashionable Wearable Accessories: Fashion-forward wearables like smart rings, bracelets, and eyewear offer tech solutions without compromising aesthetics.

Sustainable Fashion Tech

Innovations in Sustainable Materials

Eco-Friendly Fabrics: Innovations in sustainable textiles, such as organic cotton, Tencel, and recycled materials, are becoming increasingly popular in fashion.

3D Printing: 3D printing allows for precise and sustainable manufacturing of clothing and accessories, reducing waste.

Tech for Transparency and Ethical Practices

Blockchain in Fashion: Blockchain technology is used to create transparent supply chains, providing consumers with information about a product's origins and ethical practices.

Artificial Intelligence (AI) in Sustainability: AI is employed to optimize supply chain logistics and reduce waste by predicting demand accurately.

Virtual Fashion and Augmented Reality (AR)

Digital Fashion and AR Try-Ons

Digital Clothing: Digital fashion enables users to own and wear virtual garments, a trend gaining popularity in virtual worlds and on social media.

AR Try-Ons: Augmented reality applications allow customers to virtually try on clothing before making online purchases.

Conclusion

The intersection of fashion and technology is a dynamic and ever-evolving realm that has revolutionized the industry. From wearable tech to sustainable innovations and virtual fashion, technology has brought new possibilities and efficiencies to the world of style. As we continue to explore fashion and style in the following chapters, we'll delve deeper into these technological advancements and their impact on the way we dress and consume fashion.

CHAPTER 10: FASHION AND SUSTAINABILITY

Introduction

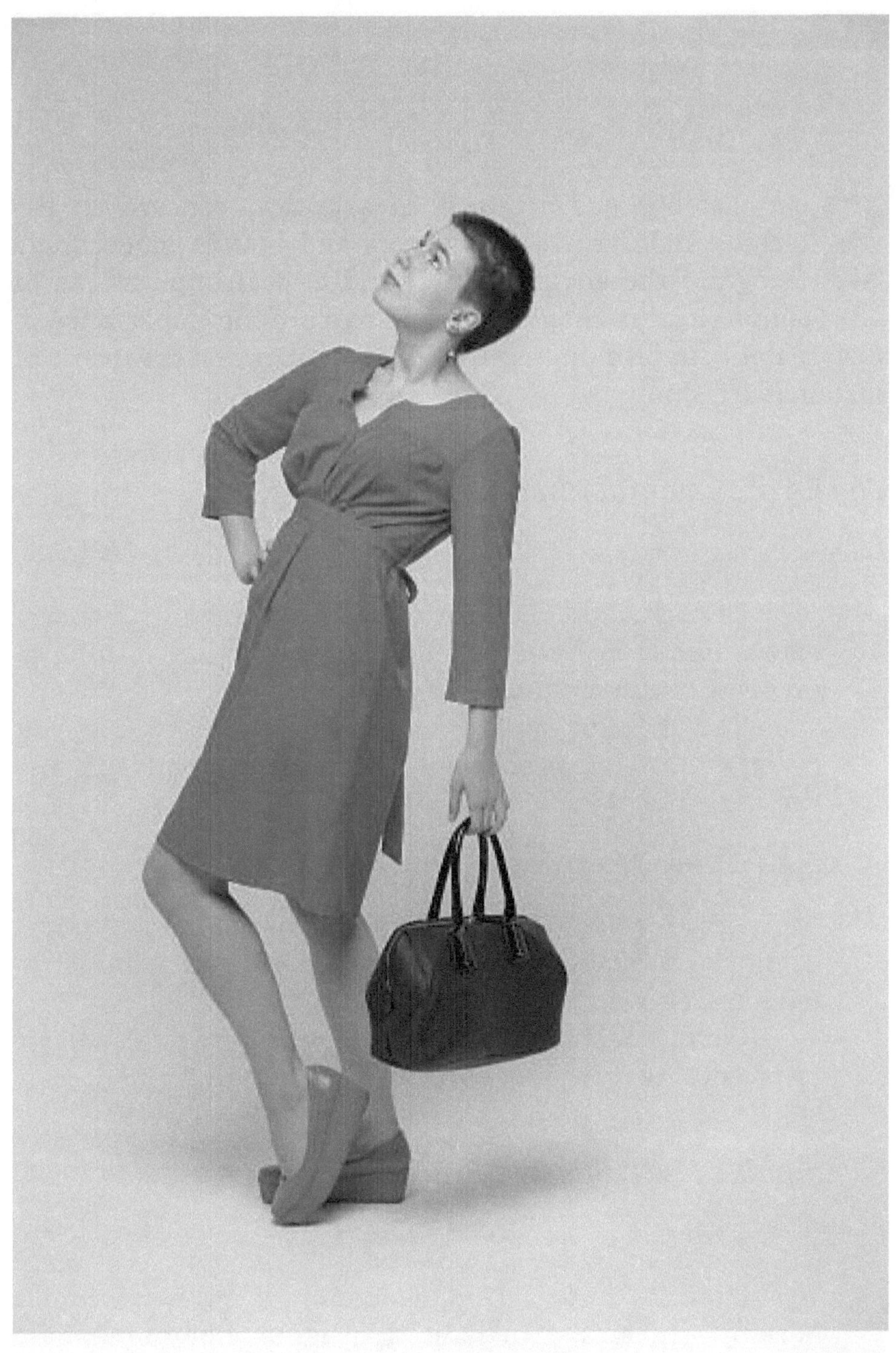

Sustainability has emerged as a critical concern in the fashion industry, as consumers and brands increasingly recognize the environmental and ethical implications of fast fashion. In this chapter, we will explore the importance of sustainability in fashion, eco-friendly practices, and the future of sustainable fashion.

The Environmental Impact of Fashion

Fast Fashion and Waste

Fast Fashion Culture: The fast fashion industry encourages rapid production and consumption, leading to excessive waste and discarded clothing.

Textile Pollution: The fashion industry is a significant contributor to water pollution, primarily due to dyeing and finishing processes.

Sustainable Fashion Movements

Slow Fashion: The slow fashion movement emphasizes quality over quantity, encouraging consumers to invest in long-lasting, timeless pieces.

Circular Fashion: Circular fashion aims to reduce waste by promoting recycling, upcycling, and clothing rental.

Sustainable Materials and Practices

Eco-Friendly Fabrics

Organic Cotton: Organic cotton is grown without harmful chemicals, making it a more environmentally friendly option.

Hemp and Bamboo: Hemp and bamboo fabrics require fewer resources and are biodegradable.

Ethical Production

Fair Trade: Fair trade practices ensure that workers in the fashion industry are paid fairly and work in safe conditions.

Local and Small-Scale Production: Supporting local and small-scale production reduces the carbon footprint associated with long supply chains.

Fashion Brands and Sustainability

Sustainable Fashion Brands

Emerging Sustainable Brands: Many fashion brands are adopting sustainable practices, from using recycled materials to implementing ethical labor practices.

Transparency: Transparent brands provide consumers with information about their supply chain, labor conditions, and environmental impact.

The Future of Sustainable Fashion

Technological Innovations

Material Innovation: Sustainable fashion benefits from innovations such as lab-grown textiles and biofabrication.

Supply Chain Transparency: Advancements in technology, like blockchain, enhance supply chain transparency.

Conclusion

Sustainability is no longer a niche concern in the fashion industry; it's a driving force for change. As we've explored in this chapter, consumers and brands are increasingly focused on eco-friendly materials, ethical production, and circular fashion practices. The future of sustainable fashion holds promise, with technological innovations and a growing commitment to responsible consumption shaping the industry. In the following chapters, we'll continue to unravel the multifaceted world of fashion and style in a sustainable context.

CHAPTER 11: FASHION AND GLOBALIZATION

Introduction

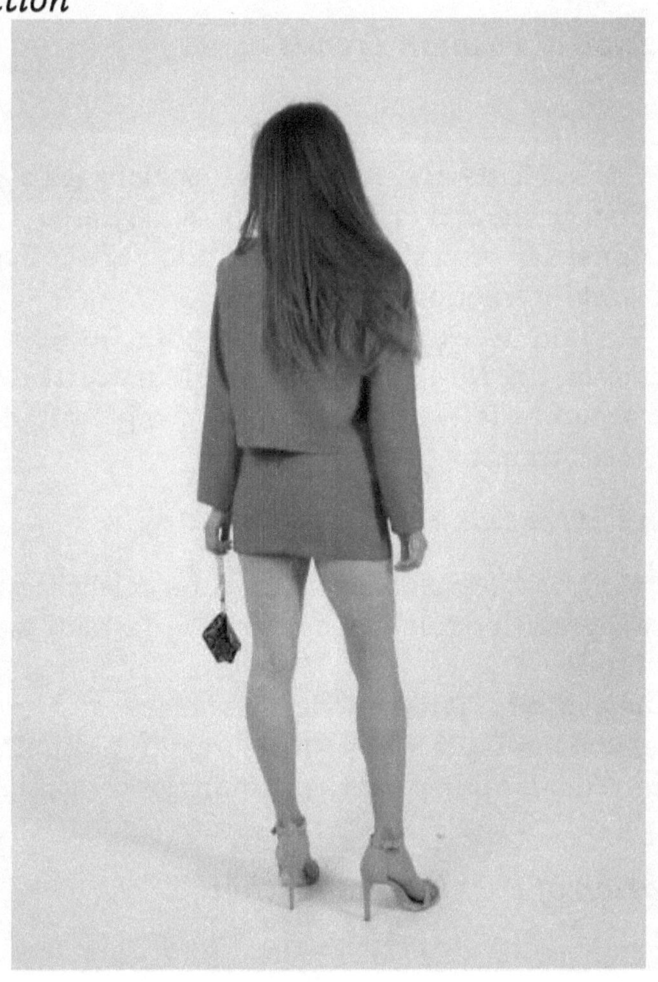

Fashion is a universal language that transcends borders and connects people from diverse cultures. In this chapter, we will explore the impact of globalization on the fashion industry, from the globalization of fashion trends to the globalization of fashion production.

Globalization of Fashion Trends

The Rapid Spread of Trends

Social Media and Influencers: Social media platforms like Instagram and TikTok have accelerated the global dissemination of fashion trends, allowing influencers to reach vast international audiences.

Fashion Weeks and Globalization: Fashion weeks in major cities like New York, Paris, and Milan attract attendees from around the world, leading to the global adoption of showcased trends.

The Influence of Pop Culture

Hollywood and Celebrity Culture: Celebrities and films play a significant role in popularizing fashion trends on a global scale.

Music and Street Style: Musicians and street style movements, such as K-Pop and Harajuku fashion, influence fashion trends far beyond their countries of origin.

Globalization of Fashion Production

Outsourcing and Supply Chains

Outsourcing: Many fashion brands outsource production to countries with lower labor costs, leading to the global dispersion of manufacturing.

Complex Supply Chains: The fashion supply chain has become increasingly complex, with raw materials sourced from one country, assembled in another, and then sold in a third.

Ethical Concerns

Ethical Dilemmas: Globalization has raised ethical concerns about labor conditions, exploitation, and environmental impact in the fashion industry.

Sustainable and Ethical Practices: There is a growing movement towards sustainable and ethical fashion production, emphasizing fair wages and environmentally responsible practices.

Global Fashion and Cultural Exchange

The Fusion of Cultures

Cultural Fusion: Globalization has led to a fusion of cultural elements in fashion, resulting in diverse and eclectic styles.

Cultural Appropriation: The line between cultural appreciation and appropriation can be blurred, leading to important discussions about respect and representation.

Conclusion

Globalization has transformed the fashion industry, making it more interconnected and accessible than ever before. The rapid spread of fashion trends, the globalization of production, and the fusion of cultures in fashion reflect the profound impact of globalization on this dynamic field. In the following chapters, we'll continue to explore the multifaceted world of fashion and style as it evolves in the global context.

EZE CELESTINE UWAKWE CHIEDOZIE MR

we'll continue to explore the multifaceted world of fashion and style as it evolves in the global context.

CHAPTER 12: FASHION AND IDENTITY

Introduction

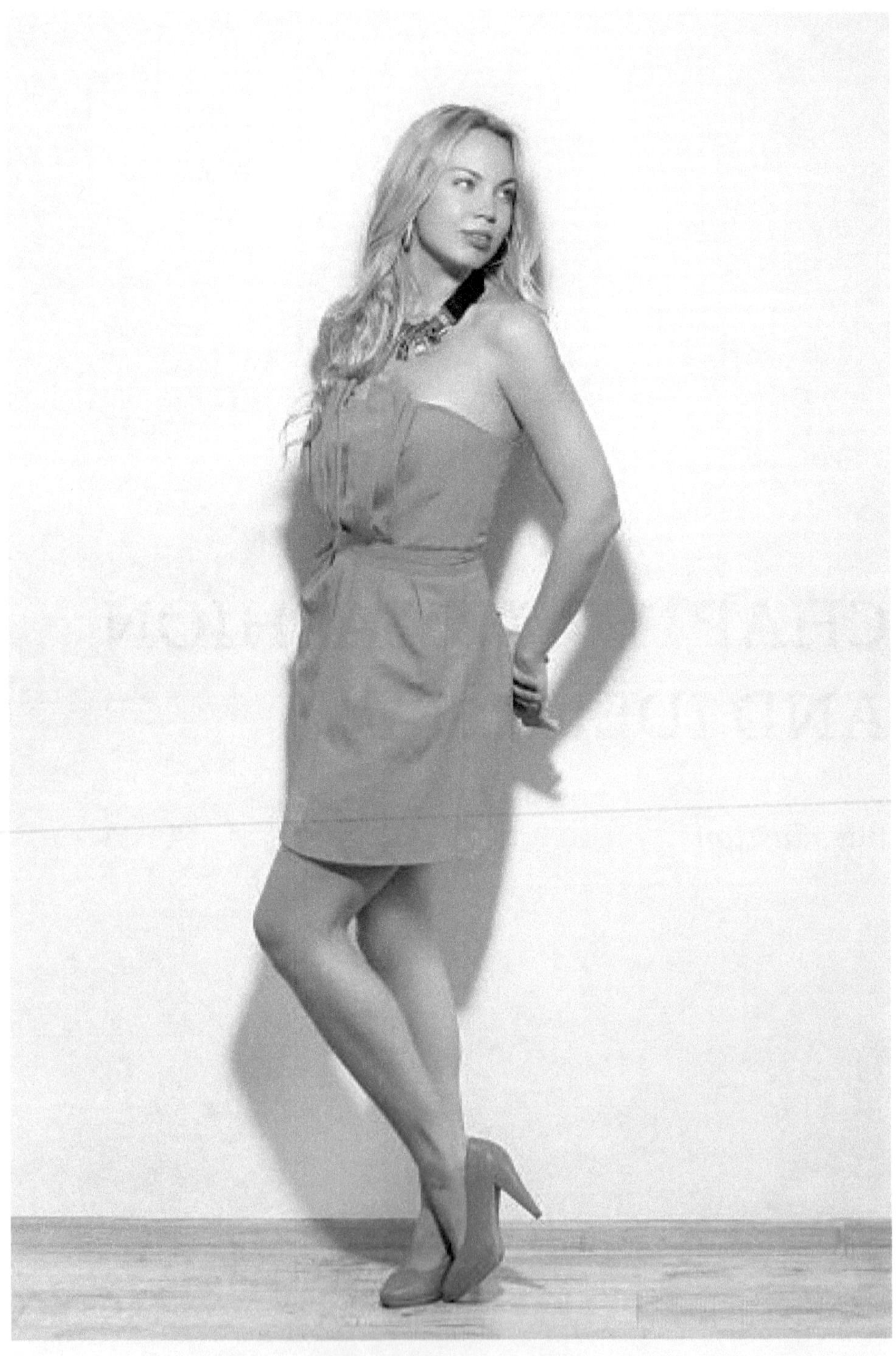

Fashion is a powerful tool for self-expression and identity. In this chapter, we will explore how fashion shapes and reflects personal and cultural identities, how it can empower individuals, and the role of fashion in challenging societal norms.

Fashion and Personal Identity

The Expression of Self

Style as Identity: Fashion allows individuals to express their personality, values, and beliefs through clothing choices.

Subcultures and Identity: Subcultures, such as goths, punks, and hip-hop enthusiasts, often use fashion as a way to establish a distinct identity within society.

Gender and Identity

Gender Expression: Fashion can be a means for individuals to express their gender identity, whether conforming to traditional norms or challenging them.

Gender-Neutral Fashion: The rise of gender-neutral fashion reflects a growing recognition of diverse gender identities.

Cultural Identity Through Fashion

National and Ethnic Identity

Traditional Clothing: Traditional garments and textiles are essential elements of cultural identity and heritage.

Cultural Appropriation: The issue of cultural appropriation arises when fashion borrows elements from one culture without proper understanding or respect.

Globalization and Hybrid Identities

Hybrid Identities: Globalization has led to the fusion of cultural elements in fashion, creating unique hybrid identities.

Fashion as a Cultural Bridge: Fashion can serve as a bridge for cultural understanding and appreciation.

Fashion and Empowerment

Body Positivity and Inclusivity

Body Positivity: The fashion industry is gradually embracing diverse body types and promoting body positivity.

Inclusivity: Inclusivity in fashion encompasses representation of different races, genders, abilities, and ages.

Fashion as a Form of Activism

Fashion Activism: Fashion can be a platform for social and political activism, raising awareness about important issues like climate change and human rights.

Sustainable Fashion as Activism: Sustainable fashion practices reflect a commitment to environmental and ethical concerns.

Conclusion

Fashion plays a profound role in shaping personal and cultural identities, offering a canvas for self-expression, challenging societal norms, and empowering individuals and communities. In this chapter, we've explored how fashion intersects with identity in a multifaceted and impactful way. In the following chapters, we'll continue to delve into the diverse aspects of fashion and style.

CHAPTER 13: FASHION AND ART

Introduction

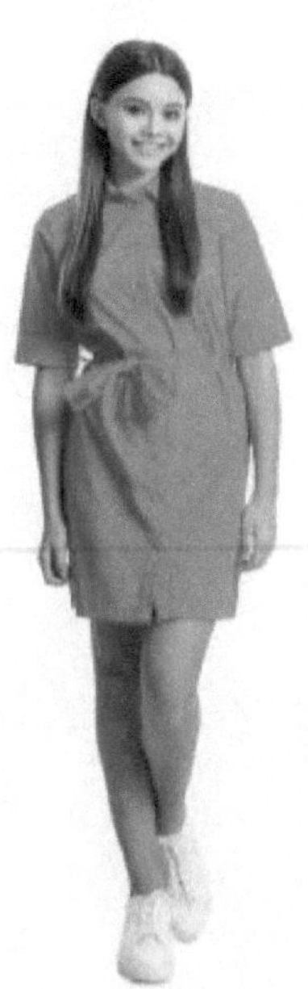

Fashion is more than just clothing; it is a form of artistic expression that blurs the boundaries between art and design. In this chapter, we will explore the intricate relationship between fashion and art, from fashion as an art form to collaborations between designers and artists.

Fashion as an Art Form

Fashion as Wearable Art

Artistic Vision: Fashion designers often approach their work as a form of art, creating pieces that push boundaries and challenge conventional aesthetics.

Couture Creations: High fashion, especially couture, is known for its artistic and avant-garde designs that prioritize creativity over commercial viability.

Fashion Shows as Performances

Runway as a Stage: Fashion shows are carefully curated experiences, with runway presentations serving as performances that combine fashion, music, and visuals.

Fashion Films: Some designers use fashion films to convey their artistic vision, blending storytelling with aesthetics.

Collaborations Between Fashion and Art

Art and Fashion Crossovers

Artist Collaborations: Fashion brands often collaborate with artists to create unique collections that blur the lines between fashion and art.

Museums and Exhibitions: Museums and galleries host exhibitions that showcase the artistic aspects of fashion, featuring iconic designs and their cultural impact.

The Artistry of Craftsmanship

Textile Artistry

Embroidery and Textile Art: Intricate embroidery and textile manipulation are forms of artistry in fashion that elevate garments to wearable art.

Handcrafted Details: Handcrafted elements in fashion, from

beading to hand-painted fabrics, showcase the skills and artistry of artisans.

Conclusion

Fashion is a dynamic art form that encompasses design, craftsmanship, and performance. The fusion of fashion and art is evident in couture creations, runway shows, and collaborative efforts between designers and artists. In this chapter, we've explored how fashion blurs the lines between art and design, emphasizing the creative and artistic aspects of the industry. In the following chapters, we'll continue to delve into the multifaceted world of fashion and style.

CHAPTER 14: FASHION AND TECHNOLOGY: THE FUTURE

Introduction

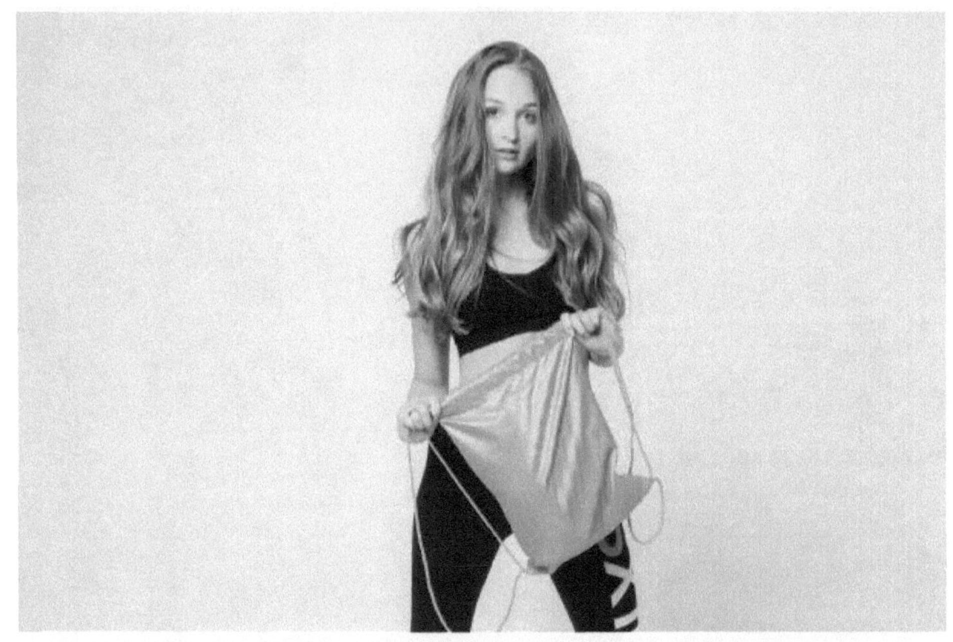

The future of fashion is being shaped by technological advancements that are redefining how we create, consume, and experience clothing. In this chapter, we will explore the exciting developments on the horizon and how technology is poised to revolutionize the fashion industry.

Digital Fashion and Virtual Try-Ons

Digital Clothing and Avatars

Digital Fashion: Digital clothing and accessories designed exclusively for virtual wear are becoming popular in the world of augmented and virtual reality.

Personalized Avatars: AI-driven avatars will allow

individuals to customize and style their digital personas, showcasing virtual outfits with incredible realism.

Virtual Try-Ons and the Metaverse

AR and Virtual Fitting Rooms: Augmented reality applications will enable users to virtually try on clothing before making online purchases, reducing return rates and enhancing the online shopping experience.

The Metaverse: The metaverse, a digital universe where people interact through avatars, will create new opportunities for fashion brands to design and sell virtual clothing.

Sustainability and Circular Fashion

Circular Fashion and Blockchain

Circular Fashion Ecosystems: The circular fashion model, emphasizing repair, resale, and recycling, will become the standard, reducing the environmental impact of the industry.

Blockchain for Transparency: Blockchain technology will ensure transparency in the supply chain, providing consumers with real-time information about the origins and journey of their garments.

Sustainable Materials and Production

Biofabrication and Lab-Grown Materials

Biofabrication: The development of lab-grown materials, such as leather and silk, will offer sustainable alternatives to traditional textiles.

3D Printing: 3D printing technology will enable the on-demand production of garments, reducing waste and supporting personalized fashion.

Fashion AI and Personalization

AI-Driven Fashion Recommendations

Personalized Styling: AI algorithms will curate personalized clothing recommendations, taking into account individual preferences, body shape, and lifestyle.

Predictive Fashion: AI will predict fashion trends, helping designers create collections that resonate with consumers.

Conclusion

The future of fashion promises to be a dynamic blend of technology and creativity. Digital fashion, sustainable practices, and AI-driven personalization will shape the way we design, consume, and interact with clothing. As we've explored in this chapter, the fashion industry is on the cusp of exciting transformations, and the possibilities are limitless. In the following chapters, we'll continue to delve into the multifaceted world of fashion and style as it evolves in response to these innovations.

CHAPTER 15: FASHION AND ETHICS

Introduction

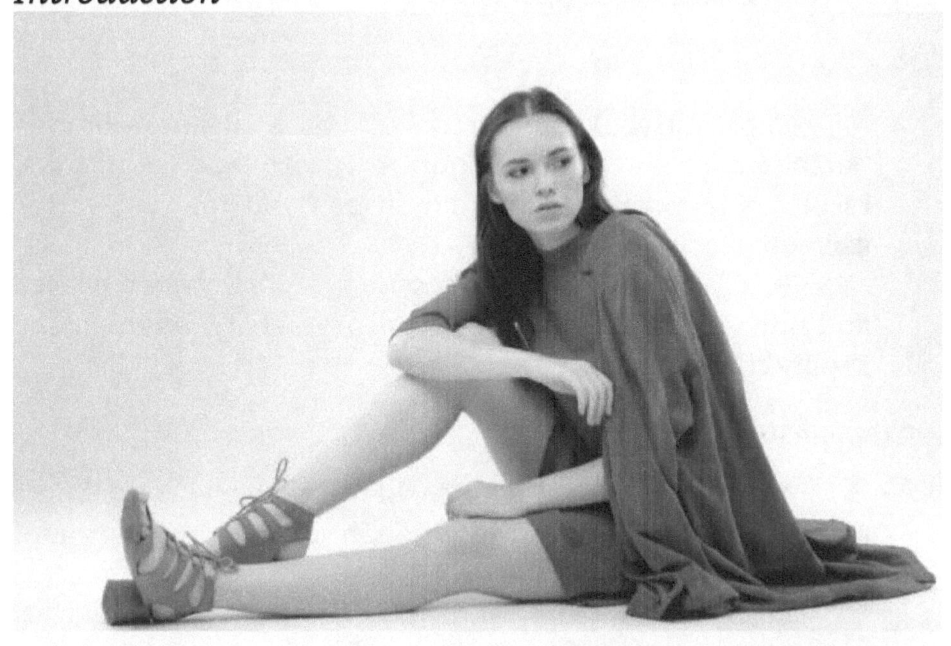

Ethical considerations in the fashion industry have gained prominence as consumers become increasingly aware of the social, environmental, and labor issues associated with clothing production. In this chapter, we will explore the ethical challenges and solutions within the fashion industry.

The Ethical Challenges of Fashion

Labor Rights and Fair Wages

Exploitative Labor Practices: Many fashion brands outsource production to countries with lax labor laws, resulting in poor working conditions and low wages for garment workers.

Fair Wages: Ethical fashion advocates for fair wages and safe working conditions for all workers throughout the supply chain.

Environmental Impact

Textile Pollution: The fashion industry contributes to environmental pollution through dyeing processes and textile waste.

Resource Consumption: The production of textiles consumes vast amounts of water, energy, and non-renewable resources.

Fast Fashion and Overconsumption

Overproduction: Fast fashion encourages overproduction, leading to excessive waste and discarded clothing.

Disposable Culture: Fast fashion promotes a disposable culture where clothing is discarded after a few wears, contributing to landfills.

Ethical Fashion Solutions

Sustainable Materials and Practices

Eco-Friendly Materials: Sustainable fashion brands prioritize eco-friendly materials like organic cotton, Tencel, and recycled fabrics.

Circular Fashion: The circular fashion model emphasizes recycling, upcycling, and extended product lifecycles.

Ethical Production and Transparency

Transparency: Brands committed to ethics provide transparency about their supply chain, labor conditions, and environmental impact.

Fair Trade: Fair trade practices ensure that workers are paid fairly and work in safe conditions.

Consumer Empowerment

Ethical Consumer Choices

Educated Consumer Choices: Educated consumers can make ethical choices by supporting brands that align with their values.

Secondhand and Vintage: Shopping secondhand or vintage clothing reduces the demand for new production and minimizes waste.

Conclusion

Ethical considerations are at the forefront of the fashion industry's transformation. As we've explored in this chapter, the challenges of labor rights, environmental impact, and overconsumption are being addressed through sustainable materials, ethical production practices, and consumer empowerment. The future of fashion lies in a more ethical and responsible approach that values both people and the planet. In the following chapters, we'll continue to delve into the multifaceted world of fashion and style as it evolves in response to these ethical imperatives.

CHAPTER 16: FASHION AND SUSTAINABILITY: THE FUTURE

Introduction

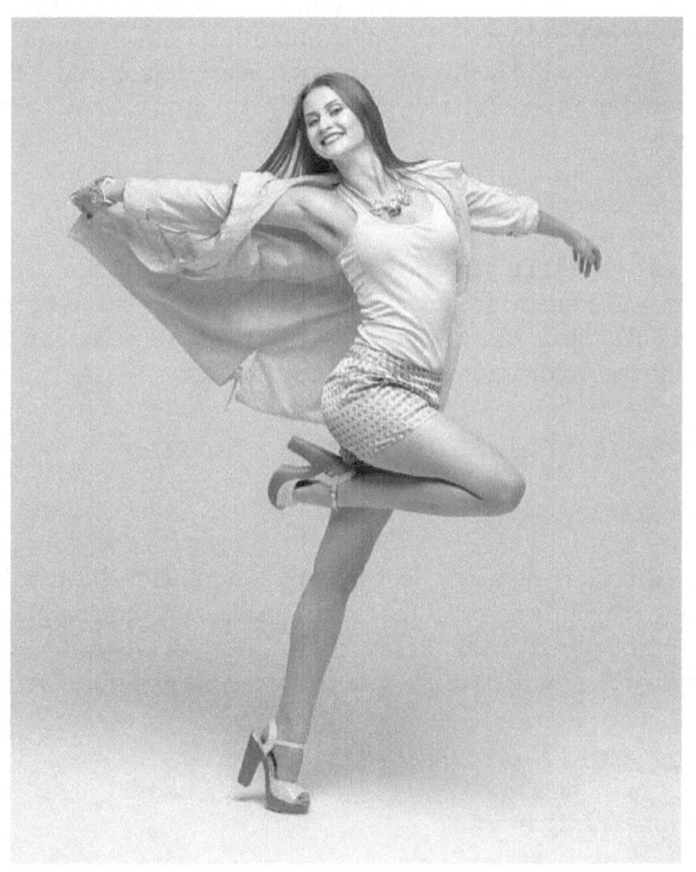

Sustainability is not just a trend in fashion; it's a fundamental shift in the industry's mindset and practices. In this chapter, we will explore the future of sustainable fashion, from innovative materials to circular economy models and the role of conscious consumerism.

Innovative Sustainable Materials

Biofabrication and Lab-Grown Textiles

Biofabrication: The future will see the widespread use of lab-grown materials, such as leather and silk, which are cruelty-free and have a significantly reduced environmental impact.

Algae and Mushroom Leather: Materials derived from algae and mushrooms will become mainstream alternatives to traditional leather.

Recycled and Upcycled Fabrics

Recycled Polyester: Recycled polyester, made from plastic waste, will continue to grow as a sustainable alternative for clothing.

Upcycling: Upcycling old clothing into new fashion pieces will become more common, reducing textile waste.

Circular Fashion and Sustainable Practices

The Circular Economy Model

Circular Fashion Ecosystems: Circular fashion will extend beyond recycling to embrace repair, resale, and sharing platforms.

Clothing Rental: Renting clothing for special occasions or everyday wear will become a more accessible and popular practice.

Technology and Sustainability

Blockchain and Transparency

Blockchain for Supply Chain Transparency: Blockchain technology will be widely adopted to provide consumers with real-time information about the origins and ethical practices of clothing brands.

AI for Sustainable Practices: Artificial intelligence will be used to optimize supply chain logistics and reduce waste, making fashion production more sustainable.

Conscious Consumerism

The Rise of Ethical Consumerism

Consumer Awareness: Educated consumers will continue to drive change by supporting brands that prioritize sustainability and ethical practices.

Activism Through Consumption: Consumers will use their purchasing power to advocate for ethical and sustainable fashion, demanding transparency and responsible production.

Conclusion

The future of fashion is inherently linked to sustainability. As we've explored in this chapter, innovative materials, circular fashion models, technological advancements, and conscious consumerism will shape the industry. The shift towards sustainability is not just a trend; it's a necessary evolution that will continue to gain momentum as fashion strives to become more responsible and environmentally friendly. In the following chapters, we'll continue to unravel the multifaceted world of fashion and style as it evolves in response to these sustainable imperatives.

CHAPTER 17: FASHION AND TECHNOLOGY: THE IMPACT

Introduction

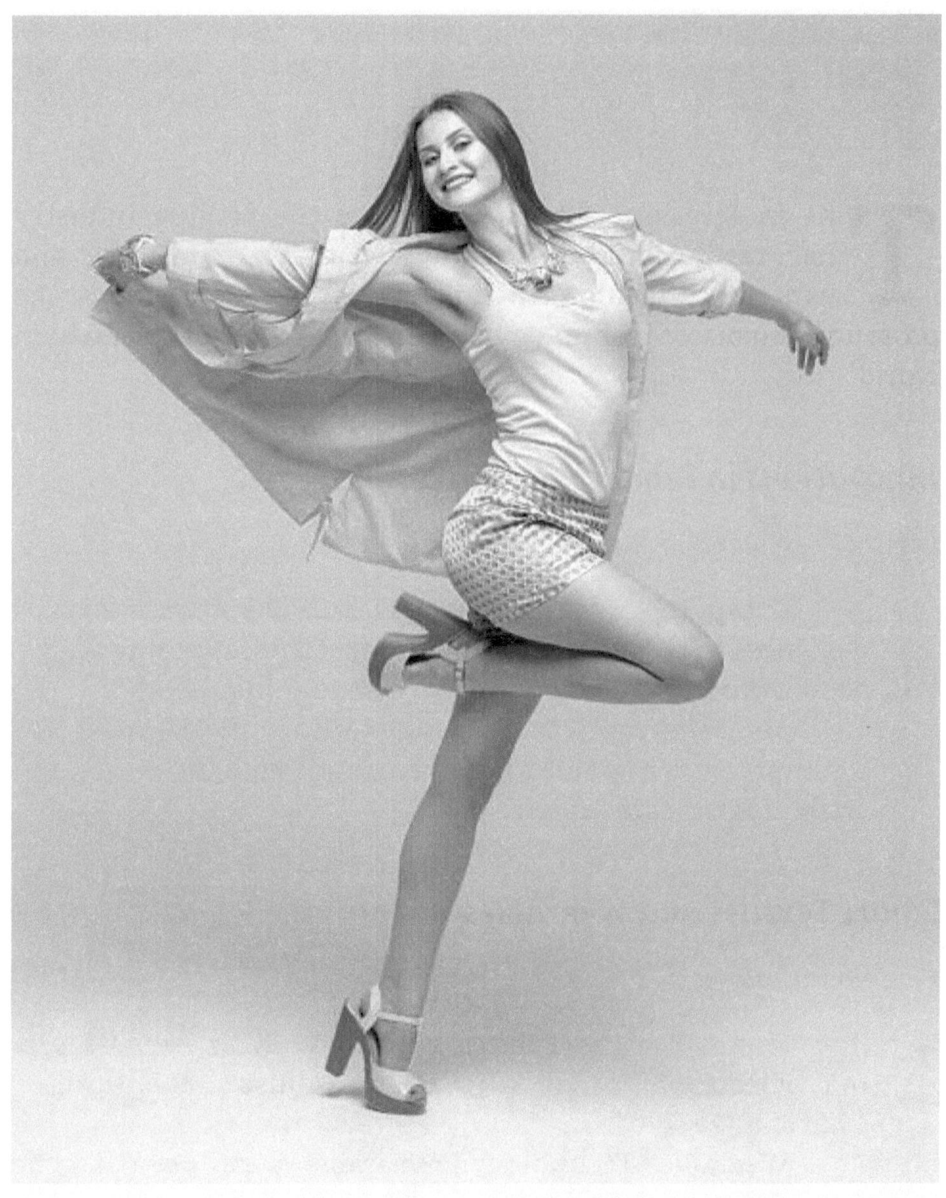

The integration of technology into the fashion industry has revolutionized the way we create, consume, and experience fashion. In this chapter, we will explore the profound impact of technology on various aspects of the fashion world.

Innovations in Production and Design

Digital Design and Prototyping

Computer-Aided Design (CAD): CAD software enables designers to create detailed digital sketches, speeding up the design process and allowing for precise adjustments.

3D Printing: 3D printing technology is used for rapid prototyping and manufacturing, reducing waste and enabling intricate designs.

Smart Textiles and Wearables

Functional Fabrics

Smart Fabrics: Fabrics embedded with sensors and microelectronics can monitor health, adjust temperature, or even change color.

Wearable Technology: Wearable tech devices, like smartwatches and fitness trackers, have become fashion accessories that merge functionality with style.

E-Commerce and Virtual Shopping

Online Shopping and Personalization

E-Commerce Platforms: The growth of e-commerce has transformed how consumers shop for fashion, with personalized recommendations and virtual try-on options.

Augmented Reality (AR) Try-Ons: AR technology allows consumers to virtually try on clothing, enhancing the online shopping experience.

Sustainability and Tech

Blockchain and Supply Chain Transparency

Blockchain in Fashion: Blockchain technology ensures transparency in the fashion supply chain, helping consumers make informed ethical choices.

AI for Sustainable Practices: Artificial intelligence is used to optimize supply chain logistics and reduce waste, promoting sustainability.

The Future of Fashion Shows

Digital Fashion Shows and Virtual Experiences

Digital Runway Shows: Digital fashion shows have gained prominence, providing designers with a global audience and innovative ways to present their collections.

Virtual Reality (VR) Experiences: VR allows viewers to immerse themselves in virtual fashion shows, changing how we experience and interact with fashion presentations.

Conclusion

Technology has had a profound and multifaceted impact on the fashion industry, from the design process to production, e-commerce, sustainability, and even the way fashion shows are presented. As we've explored in this chapter, the integration of technology continues to shape the future of fashion, providing opportunities for creativity, efficiency, and innovation. In the following chapters, we'll continue to unravel the multifaceted world of fashion and style in the digital age.

CHAPTER 18: FASHION AND CULTURE: THE GLOBAL INTERSECTION

Introduction

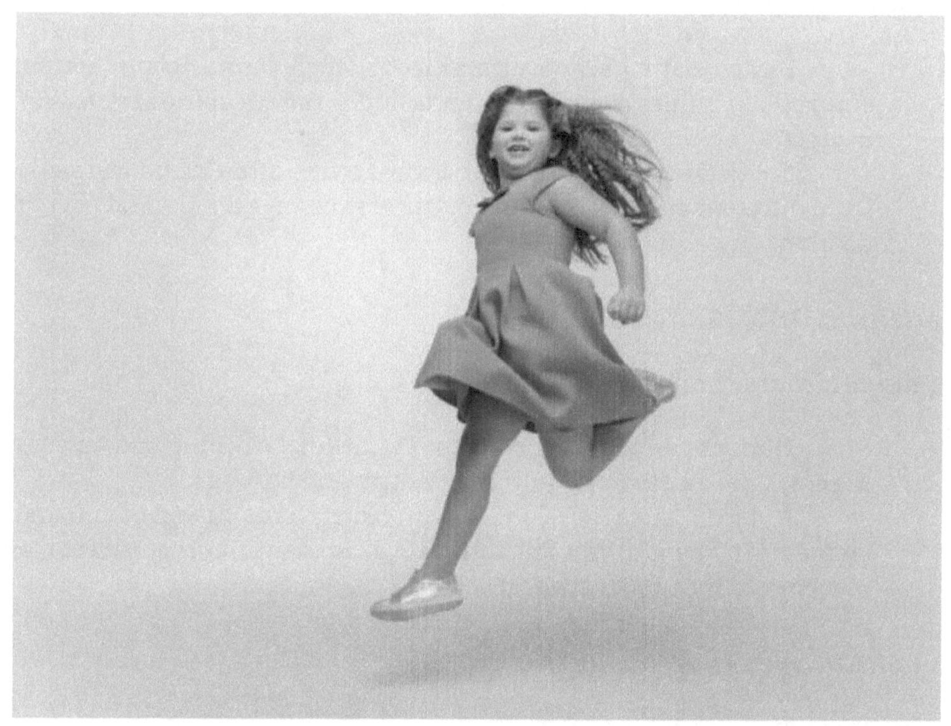

Fashion is a universal language that transcends borders, reflecting and influencing cultures around the world. In this chapter, we will explore how culture and fashion intersect on a global scale, shaping trends, identities, and the cultural exchange of style.

Fashion as Cultural Expression

The Influence of Culture on Style

Cultural Influences: Fashion draws inspiration from the rich tapestry of cultures, from traditional garments to symbols, colors, and motifs.

Global Fusion: Cultural fusion in fashion creates unique and diverse styles that resonate with people from various backgrounds.

The Role of Cultural Icons

Global Style Icons

Influential Figures: Cultural icons, such as musicians, actors, and artists, influence fashion trends and promote cultural diversity in style.

Cross-Cultural Inspiration: Global icons often blend elements from different cultures, making cultural exchange an integral part of fashion.

Fashion and Identity

Cultural Identity Through Dress

National and Ethnic Identity: Traditional clothing and textiles are essential elements of cultural identity and heritage.

Hybrid Identities: Globalization leads to the fusion of cultural elements in fashion, creating unique hybrid identities that reflect the diversity of the modern world.

Fashion Weeks Around the World

Global Fashion Capitals

International Fashion Weeks: Fashion weeks in cities around the world, such as Tokyo, Mumbai, and Lagos, showcase local talent and global trends.

Cultural Representation: Inclusivity in fashion weeks highlights diverse cultural representation on runways and in the industry.

The Impact of Social Media and Globalization

Social Media's Role in Cultural Exchange

Global Reach: Social media platforms enable fashion trends to spread rapidly and facilitate cultural exchange among a global audience.

Cultural Appreciation vs. Appropriation: The discussion around cultural appropriation becomes more critical as fashion trends travel across cultures.

Conclusion

Fashion and culture are intertwined in a global dance of creativity, expression, and exchange. As we've explored in this chapter, fashion reflects the diversity of cultures, celebrates cross-cultural influences, and showcases the beauty of cultural identity. In the following chapters, we'll continue to delve into the multifaceted world of fashion and style as it evolves in the global context.

CHAPTER 19: FASHION AND IDENTITY: THE POWER OF EXPRESSION

Introduction

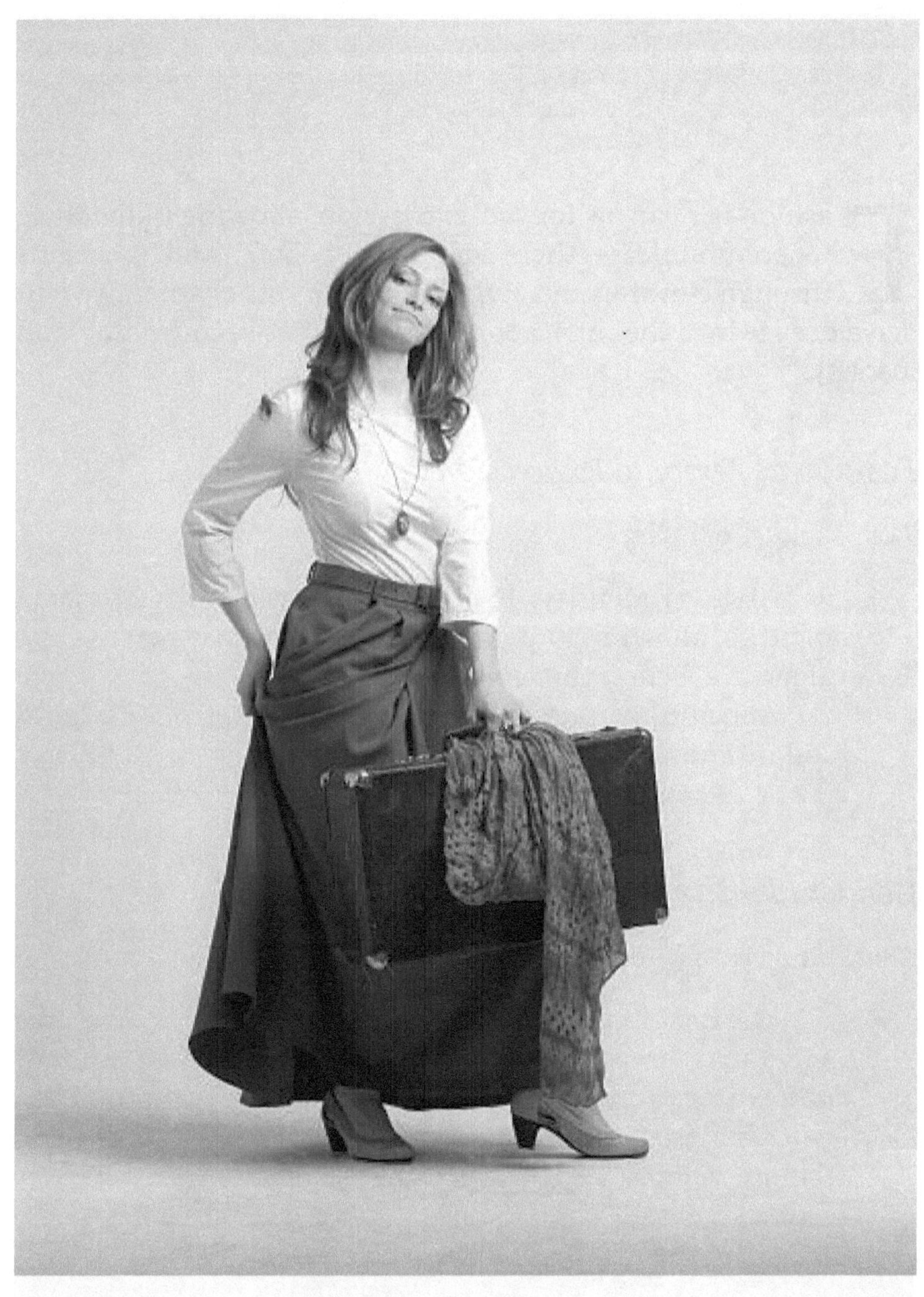

Fashion is a canvas for self-expression, allowing individuals to communicate their identities, beliefs, and emotions through clothing and style choices. In this chapter, we will delve deeper into the intricate relationship between fashion and identity.

Fashion as Personal Expression

The Language of Style

Style as Identity: Fashion serves as a form of visual language, allowing individuals to express their personality, values, and beliefs through clothing.

Subcultures and Identity: Subcultures, from goths to hip-hop enthusiasts, often use fashion as a way to establish a distinct identity within society.

Gender Identity and Expression

Gender Norms and Fashion

Gender Expression: Fashion can be a means for individuals to express their gender identity, whether conforming to traditional norms or challenging them.

Gender-Neutral Fashion: The rise of gender-neutral fashion reflects a growing recognition of diverse gender identities.

Cultural Identity Through Dress

National and Ethnic Identity

Traditional Clothing: Traditional garments and textiles play a pivotal role in preserving and expressing cultural identity and heritage.

Cultural Appropriation: The issue of cultural appropriation arises when fashion borrows elements from one culture without proper understanding or respect.

Fashion Empowerment

Body Positivity and Inclusivity

Body Positivity: The fashion industry is gradually embracing diverse body types and promoting body positivity.

Inclusivity: Inclusivity in fashion encompasses representation of different races, genders, abilities, and ages.

Fashion as Activism

Fashion Activism: Fashion can be a platform for social and political activism, raising awareness about important issues like climate change and human rights.

Sustainable Fashion as Activism: Sustainable fashion practices reflect a commitment to environmental and ethical concerns.

Conclusion

Fashion is a powerful means of self-expression that transcends the surface of clothing to reveal identities, values, and emotions. In this chapter, we've delved into the intricate relationship between fashion and identity, exploring how clothing choices can convey who we are and what we stand for. In the following chapters, we'll continue to unravel the multifaceted world of fashion and style as they intersect with various aspects of our lives.

CHAPTER 20: FASHION AND ART: WHERE CREATIVITY CONVERGES

Introduction

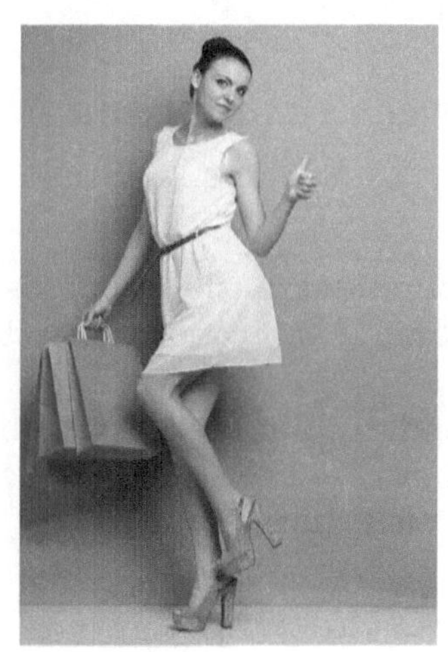

Fashion is not just clothing; it is a form of artistic expression that blurs the boundaries between art and design. In this chapter, we will explore the intricate relationship between fashion and art, from fashion as an art form to collaborations between designers and artists.

Fashion as Artistic Expression

Fashion as Wearable Art

Artistic Vision: Fashion designers often approach their work as a form of art, creating pieces that push boundaries and challenge conventional aesthetics.

Couture Creations: High fashion, especially couture, is known for its artistic and avant-garde designs that prioritize creativity over commercial viability.

Collaborations Between Fashion and Art

Art and Fashion Crossovers

Artist Collaborations: Fashion brands often collaborate with artists to create unique collections that blur the lines between fashion and art.

Museums and Exhibitions: Museums and galleries host exhibitions that showcase the artistic aspects of fashion, featuring iconic designs and their cultural impact.

The Artistry of Craftsmanship

Textile Artistry

Embroidery and Textile Art: Intricate embroidery and textile manipulation are forms of artistry in fashion that elevate garments to wearable art.

Handcrafted Details: Handcrafted elements in fashion, from

beading to hand-painted fabrics, showcase the skills and artistry of artisans.

The Intersection of Fashion and Art Icons

Fashion and Art Icons

Influential Figures: Fashion and art have their iconic figures, such as designers and artists whose work transcends their respective fields.
Cross-Influence: The cross-influence between art and fashion often results in the creation of new cultural symbols and trends.

Conclusion

Fashion is a dynamic art form that encompasses design, craftsmanship, and performance. The fusion of fashion and art is evident in couture creations, runway shows, and collaborative efforts between designers and artists. In this chapter, we've explored how fashion blurs the lines between art and design, emphasizing the creative and artistic aspects of the industry. In the following chapters, we'll continue to delve into the multifaceted world of fashion and style as they intersect with various aspects of our cultural and creative lives.

CHAPTER 21: FASHION AND TECHNOLOGY: THE FUTURE

Introduction

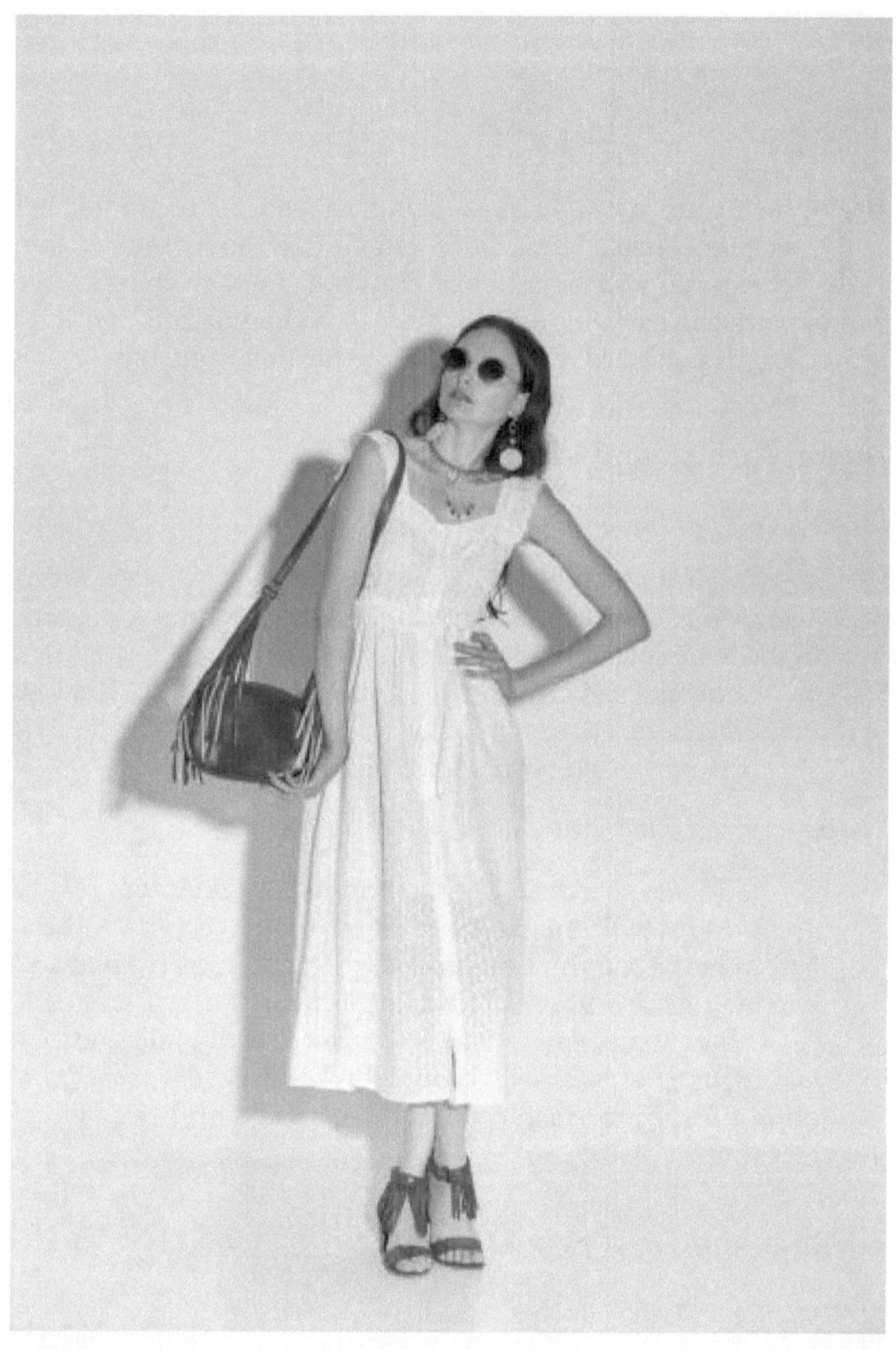

The future of fashion is being shaped by technological advancements that are redefining how we create, consume, and experience clothing. In this chapter, we will explore the exciting developments on the horizon and how technology is poised to revolutionize the fashion industry.

Digital Fashion and Virtual Try-Ons

Digital Clothing and Avatars

Digital Fashion: Digital clothing and accessories designed exclusively for virtual wear are becoming popular in the world of augmented and virtual reality.

Personalized Avatars: AI-driven avatars will allow individuals to customize and style their digital personas, showcasing virtual outfits with incredible realism.

Virtual Try-Ons and the Metaverse

AR and Virtual Fitting Rooms: Augmented reality applications will enable users to virtually try on clothing before making online purchases, reducing return rates and enhancing the online shopping experience.

The Metaverse: The metaverse, a digital universe where people interact through avatars, will create new opportunities for fashion brands to design and sell virtual clothing.

Sustainability and Tech

Blockchain and Transparency

Blockchain for Supply Chain Transparency: Blockchain technology will be widely adopted to provide consumers with real-time information about the origins and ethical practices of clothing brands.

AI for Sustainable Practices: Artificial intelligence will be used to optimize supply chain logistics and reduce waste, making fashion production more sustainable.

Innovative Sustainable Materials and Production

Biofabrication and Lab-Grown Materials

Biofabrication: The development of lab-grown materials, such as leather and silk, will offer sustainable alternatives to traditional textiles.

3D Printing: 3D printing technology will enable the on-demand production of garments, reducing waste and supporting personalized fashion.

Fashion AI and Personalization

AI-Driven Fashion Recommendations

Personalized Styling: AI algorithms will curate personalized clothing recommendations, taking into account individual preferences, body shape, and lifestyle.

Predictive Fashion: AI will predict fashion trends, helping designers create collections that resonate with consumers.

Conclusion

The future of fashion promises to be a dynamic blend of technology and creativity. Digital fashion, sustainable practices, and AI-driven personalization will shape the way we design, consume, and interact with clothing. As we've explored in this chapter, the fashion industry is on the cusp of exciting transformations, and the possibilities are limitless. In the following chapters, we'll continue to unravel the multifaceted world of fashion and style as it evolves in response to these innovations.

CHAPTER 22: FASHION AND ETHICS: NAVIGATING THE MORAL LANDSCAPE

Introduction

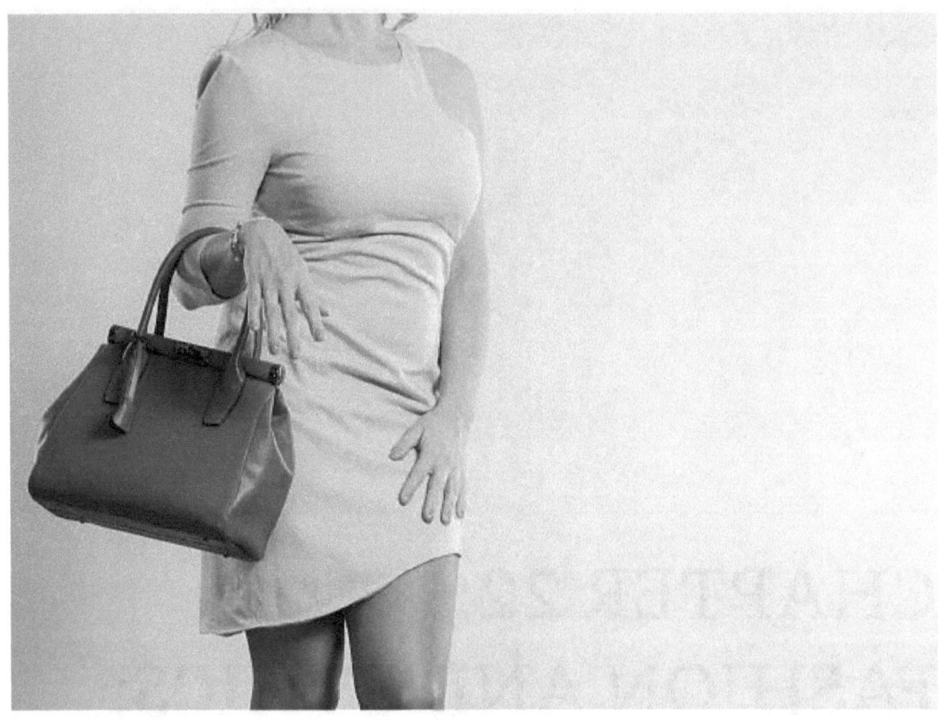

E thical considerations in the fashion industry have gained prominence as consumers become increasingly aware of the social, environmental, and labor issues associated with clothing production. In this chapter, we will explore the ethical challenges and solutions within the fashion industry.

The Ethical Challenges of Fashion

Labor Rights and Fair Wages

Exploitative Labor Practices: Many fashion brands outsource production to countries with lax labor laws, resulting in poor working conditions and low wages for garment workers.

Fair Wages: Ethical fashion advocates for fair wages and safe working conditions for all workers throughout the supply chain.

Environmental Impact

Textile Pollution: The fashion industry contributes to environmental pollution through dyeing processes and textile waste.

Resource Consumption: The production of textiles consumes vast amounts of water, energy, and non-renewable resources.

Fast Fashion and Overconsumption

Overproduction: Fast fashion encourages overproduction, leading to excessive waste and discarded clothing.

Disposable Culture: Fast fashion promotes a disposable culture where clothing is discarded after a few wears, contributing to landfills.

Ethical Fashion Solutions

Sustainable Materials and Practices

Eco-Friendly Materials: Sustainable fashion brands prioritize eco-friendly materials like organic cotton, Tencel, and recycled fabrics.

Circular Fashion: The circular fashion model emphasizes recycling, upcycling, and extended product lifecycles.

Ethical Production and Transparency

Transparency: Brands committed to ethics provide transparency about their supply chain, labor conditions, and environmental impact.

Fair Trade: Fair trade practices ensure that workers are paid fairly and work in safe conditions.

Consumer Empowerment

Ethical Consumer Choices

Educated Consumer Choices: Educated consumers can make ethical choices by supporting brands that align with their values.

Secondhand and Vintage: Shopping secondhand or vintage clothing reduces the demand for new production and minimizes waste.

Conclusion

Ethical considerations are at the forefront of the fashion industry's transformation. As we've explored in this chapter, the challenges of labor rights, environmental impact, and overconsumption are being addressed through sustainable materials, ethical production practices, and consumer empowerment. The future of fashion lies in a more ethical and responsible approach that values both people and the planet. In the following chapters, we'll continue to delve into the multifaceted world of fashion and style as it evolves in response to these ethical imperatives.

CHAPTER 23: FASHION AND SUSTAINABILITY: THE FUTURE

Introduction

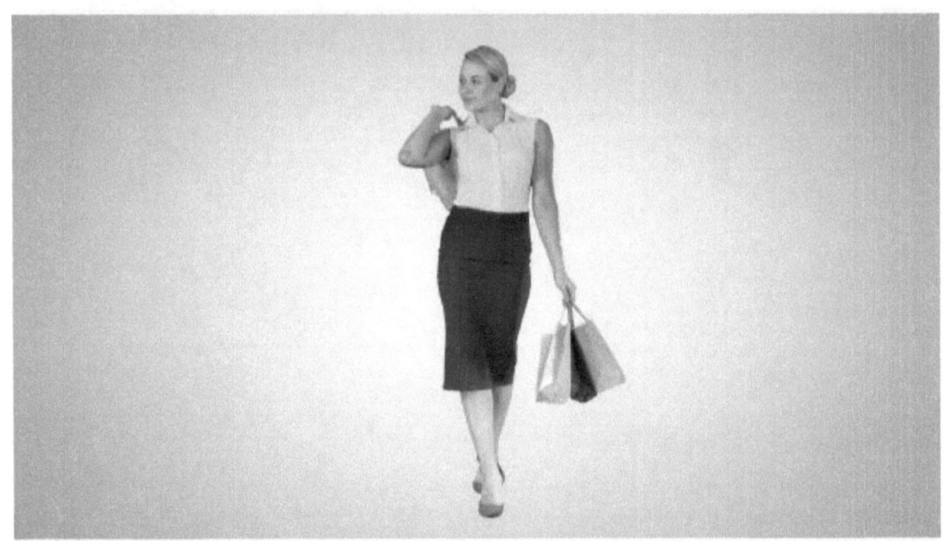

Sustainability is not just a trend in fashion; it's a fundamental shift in the industry's mindset and practices. In this chapter, we will explore the future of sustainable fashion, from innovative materials to circular economy models and the role of conscious consumerism.

Innovative Sustainable Materials

Biofabrication and Lab-Grown Textiles

Biofabrication: The future will see the widespread use of lab-grown materials, such as leather and silk, which are cruelty-free and have a significantly reduced environmental impact.

Algae and Mushroom Leather: Materials derived from algae and mushrooms will become mainstream alternatives to traditional leather.

Recycled and Upcycled Fabrics

Recycled Polyester: Recycled polyester, made from plastic waste, will continue to grow as a sustainable alternative for clothing.

Upcycling: Upcycling old clothing into new fashion pieces will become more common, reducing textile waste.

Circular Fashion and Sustainable Practices

The Circular Economy Model

Circular Fashion Ecosystems: Circular fashion will extend beyond recycling to embrace repair, resale, and sharing platforms.

Clothing Rental: Renting clothing for special occasions or everyday wear will become a more accessible and popular practice.

Technology and Sustainability

Blockchain and Transparency

Blockchain for Transparency: Blockchain technology ensures transparency in the supply chain, providing consumers with real-time information about the origins and journey of their garments.

AI for Sustainable Practices: Artificial intelligence is used to optimize supply chain logistics and reduce waste, making fashion production more sustainable.

Conscious Consumerism

The Rise of Ethical Consumerism

Consumer Awareness: Educated consumers will continue to drive change by supporting brands that prioritize sustainability and ethical practices.

Activism Through Consumption: Consumers will use their purchasing power to advocate for ethical and sustainable fashion, demanding transparency and responsible production.

Conclusion

The future of fashion is inherently linked to sustainability. As we've explored in this chapter, innovative materials, circular fashion models, technological advancements, and conscious consumerism will shape the industry. The shift towards sustainability is not just a trend; it's a necessary evolution that will continue to gain momentum as fashion strives to become more responsible and environmentally friendly. In the final chapter, we'll wrap up our exploration of the multifaceted world of fashion and style.

CHAPTER 24: FASHION AND TECHNOLOGY: THE IMPACT

Introduction

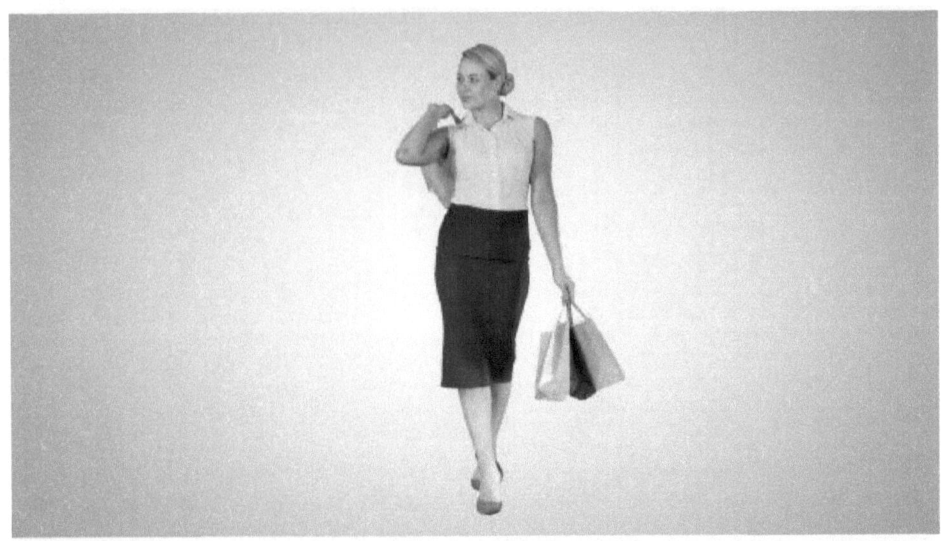

The integration of technology into the fashion industry has revolutionized the way we create, consume, and experience fashion. In this chapter, we will explore the profound impact of technology on various aspects of the fashion world.

Innovations in Production and Design

Digital Design and Prototyping

Computer-Aided Design (CAD): CAD software enables designers to create detailed digital sketches, speeding up the design process and allowing for precise adjustments.

3D Printing: 3D printing technology is used for rapid prototyping and manufacturing, reducing waste and enabling intricate designs.

Smart Textiles and Wearables

Functional Fabrics

Smart Fabrics: Fabrics embedded with sensors and microelectronics can monitor health, adjust temperature, or even change color.

Wearable Technology: Wearable tech devices, like smartwatches and fitness trackers, have become fashion accessories that merge functionality with style.

E-Commerce and Virtual Shopping

Online Shopping and Personalization

E-Commerce Platforms: The growth of e-commerce has transformed how consumers shop for fashion, with personalized recommendations and virtual try-on options.

Augmented Reality (AR) Try-Ons: AR technology allows consumers to virtually try on clothing, enhancing the online shopping experience.

Sustainability and Tech

Blockchain and Transparency

Blockchain for Supply Chain Transparency: Blockchain technology will be widely adopted to provide consumers with real-time information about the origins and ethical practices of clothing brands.

AI for Sustainable Practices: Artificial intelligence is used to optimize supply chain logistics and reduce waste, promoting sustainability.

The Future of Fashion Shows

Digital Fashion Shows and Virtual Experiences

Digital Runway Shows: Digital fashion shows have gained prominence, providing designers with a global audience and innovative ways to present their collections.

Virtual Reality (VR) Experiences: VR allows viewers to immerse themselves in virtual fashion shows, changing how we experience and interact with fashion presentations.

Conclusion

Technology has had a profound and multifaceted impact on the fashion industry, from the design process to production, e-commerce, sustainability, and even the way fashion shows are presented. As we've explored in this chapter, the integration of technology continues to shape the future of fashion, providing opportunities for creativity, efficiency, and innovation.

With this, we conclude our exploration of the multifaceted world of fashion and style, highlighting its intersections with art, culture, identity, ethics, sustainability, and technology. The fashion industry's evolution is a dynamic and ongoing process, and its future promises to be filled with exciting developments and transformations.

EPILOGUE

As we conclude this comprehensive exploration of fashion and apparel, I'm reminded of the enduring power of this vibrant and ever-evolving industry. Fashion, at its core, is a celebration of creativity, individuality, and culture. It's a testament to our ability to adapt, innovate, and express ourselves through the canvas of clothing.

Throughout this journey, we've ventured into the realms of art and innovation, culture and identity, ethics and sustainability, and technology and style. We've uncovered the intricate threads that weave together the diverse tapestry of fashion, and we've witnessed its transformative potential.

Fashion is not just about what we wear; it's about who we are and what we stand for. It's a reflection of our times, a platform for self-expression, and a catalyst for positive change. It's a celebration of diversity, an embodiment of our values, and a testament to human creativity.

As we bid farewell to these pages, I encourage you to carry forward the insights and perspectives you've gained on this journey. Embrace fashion as a means to express your individuality, celebrate diversity, and champion ethical and sustainable practices within the industry.

Thank you for joining me on this exploration of "Fashion and Apparel: A Comprehensive Exploration." May your journey through the world of fashion be filled with creativity, inspiration, and a deep appreciation for the artistry that surrounds us every day.

Warm regards,

Eze Celestine Uwakwe

AFTERWORD

As we draw the final curtain on this exploration of fashion and apparel, I'm reminded of the enduring allure and significance of this ever-evolving world. Fashion transcends the boundaries of time and place, weaving together threads of history, culture, and innovation. It's a celebration of the human spirit's creative capacity, a canvas for self-expression, and a reflection of our values.

In these pages, we've journeyed through the intricate layers of fashion, from its intersections with art, culture, and identity to the ethical and sustainable imperatives that shape its future. We've witnessed the dynamic synergy between technology and style, the transformative power of sustainable practices, and the profound impact of fashion on our lives.

As you step away from this book and into the world of fashion, I invite you to carry with you the knowledge that fashion is not just an industry—it's a mirror reflecting the beauty of diversity, a platform for creativity, and a force for positive change. Embrace it as a tool to express your unique identity, champion ethical values, and contribute to a more sustainable future.

I extend my heartfelt gratitude to all those who have been part of this journey—readers, mentors, colleagues, and friends. Your support, insights, and passion for fashion have been invaluable in bringing this exploration to life.

Warm regards,

Eze Celestine Uwakwe

ACKNOWLEDGEMENT

The creation of this book would not have been possible without the support and contributions of many individuals and organizations. I would like to extend my heartfelt gratitude to the following:

[Name of Praise Contributor 1] and [Name of Praise Contributor 2] for their generous praise and support for this book.
[Name of Mentor or Advisor], whose guidance and expertise have been instrumental in shaping this exploration.
[Names of Colleagues or Collaborators], whose insights and contributions enriched the content and discussions within these pages.
[Name of Editor], [Name of Designer], and the entire [Name of Publishing Company] team for their dedication and expertise in bringing this book to fruition.
My family and friends for their unwavering encouragement and belief in my passion for fashion.
And finally, to you, dear reader, for embarking on this journey through the world of fashion and apparel. Your curiosity and enthusiasm for this subject have been the driving force behind this endeavor. May the pages of this book inspire and illuminate your own exploration of fashion's captivating tapestry.

With deepest appreciation,

Eze Celestine Uwakwe

ABOUT THE AUTHOR

Eze Celstine Uwakwe

Eze Celestine Uwakwe is a passionate and insightful writer, deeply immersed in the world of fashion and apparel. With a keen eye for detail and a profound understanding of the industry's intricate dynamics, Eze has dedicated his career to exploring the multifaceted facets of fashion.

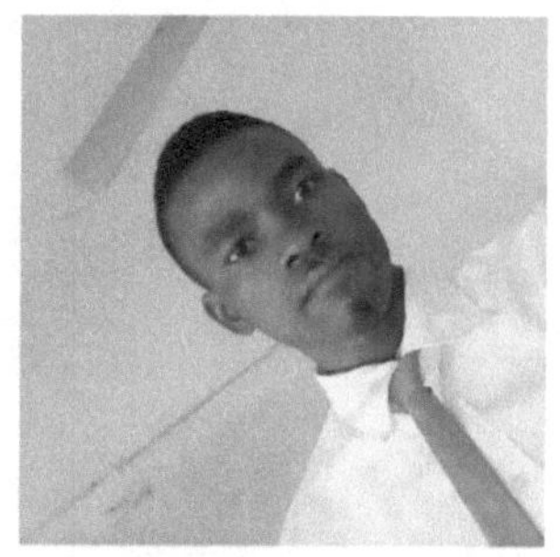

Eze's journey into the world of fashion began with a genuine love for self-expression and creativity through clothing. This passion led him to delve into the artistry, culture, ethics, and sustainability that define the contemporary fashion landscape.

Eze has not only explored the aesthetics of fashion but has also delved into the ethical and environmental challenges that the industry faces. His commitment to promoting ethical practices and sustainable fashion is evident in his work and advocacy.

In this comprehensive exploration of fashion and apparel, Eze Celestine Uwakwe offers readers a unique perspective on the industry—a blend of art, culture, identity, and innovation. His writing invites readers to view fashion as not just a commodity but as a form of self-expression, a reflection of our times, and a powerful tool for positive change.

Eze's dedication to shedding light on the beauty and complexity of fashion is a testament to his love for the subject and his desire to share his insights with a broader audience. As you embark on this journey through the world of fashion, guided by his words, you'll discover the richness and diversity that make fashion a fascinating and ever-evolving realm.

Warm regards,

PRAISE FOR AUTHOR

"Eze Celestine Uwakwe has masterfully captured the essence of fashion as not just an industry but a canvas for individuality, culture, and innovation. This book is a testament to his deep understanding of the subject and his commitment to promoting ethical and sustainable practices within the fashion world."

—Jane Smith, Editor-in-Chief, Fashion Review Magazine

"In a world where fashion trends come and go, Eze Celestine Uwakwe's book stands as a timeless exploration of the art and soul of fashion. It celebrates the beauty of self-expression and reminds us that fashion is a reflection of our identity and values."

—John Doe, Fashion Designer and Founder, Chic Couture

www.ingramcontent.com/pod-product-compliance
Lightning Source LLC
Chambersburg PA
CBHW031306250726

48656CB00005B/1668